Mildred & Jim Hurley
Jan 19, 1961
1030 Parkside place
Lindsay, Calif.

Mildred & Jim Hurley
Jan 19, 1961
1030 Parkside place
Lindsay, Calif.

CARY MIDDLECOFF'S
MASTER
GUIDE
TO
GOLF

Also by Cary Middlecoff

ADVANCED GOLF

CARY MIDDLECOFF'S

DELUXE EDITION

Edited by TOM MICHAEL

Illustrations by EDWARD O. BAILEY

MASTER
GUIDE
TO
GOLF

PRENTICE-HALL, INC., ENGLEWOOD CLIFFS, N.J.

APPROACH TO THE GAME

I assume, since you are starting to read this book, that you either, 1. want to learn how to play golf, or, 2. want to learn MORE about how to play golf. Whichever is the case, I commend you. You are involving yourself in what I believe to be the best game ever devised by man.

The pleasures of golf are endless. (Its frustrations are endless, too, but that fact only serves to heighten the pleasures when they come.) To hit a golf ball solidly on the face of a club and see the ball take off on a good, clean line for the pin is to enjoy one of life's more satisfying experiences. The same may be said of hitting a truly-gauged putt and seeing it disappear into the cup. If either of these are the means of defeating a staunch opponent, so much the better. But the great satisfaction is there regardless of the circumstances.

A wonderful part of the game is that these feats are within the capabilities of all golfers. There is no dub so inept that now and again he will not hit a shot or hole a putt that an Open Champion can envy. These good shots come more often to the better players, true, but they come to all. And when they come to the dub, they delight him more because he hits them less often.

It is one of golf's great beauties that it provides competitive levels for every man, woman and child who plays. Whether you shoot 150 for 18 holes or less than half that, you can virtually always find someone about your own speed—and who is glad to tee off against you for just that reason. Nor is it at all necessary that you be evenly matched in ability with your opponents. Golf has a most admirable handicap system. Ask or give a few handicap strokes and tee right off. If the handicap proves wrong, it is easily adjusted.

Golf's appeal is to all types, all ages. There are among my friends men and women past 70 who play the game with as much zest as I do. Children are coming more and more to play golf, and as I see them doing so it makes me feel good to realize that they are learning a game they can play with pleasure through life. No particular type of personality is needed to enjoy golf. I see foursomes who laugh and joke their way around the golf course. I see foursomes who play the game in virtual silence and with grim intensity. I can detect no difference in the amount of enjoyment derived by each.

It is wonderful fun to get out on a course with a congenial bunch and compete fiercely. It is likewise wonderful fun to go off alone to the practice tee and bang out shots in solitude. I see husband and wife enjoying the game together. Few games can make this claim.

Furthermore, the game is health-giving. A good, brisk walk in the open air helps us all. Golf courses, moreover, are beautiful. Some are more beautiful than others, but all of the thousands I have seen have beauty.

One of the best things of all about golf is that it always offers room for improvement. There was never a round so good but that it could have been bettered by a straighter drive here, a more intelligently played iron shot there, a more accurately gauged putt somewhere along the line. Conversely, there was never a round so bad but that it contained a few decent shots—shots showing promise of a better day in the future.

Best of all, the 150 shooter gets just as much satisfaction out of lowering his average score by five strokes as the 80-shooter does. Improvement is a great source of satisfaction for us all. Nor does one ever become too old to learn something new about golf. You may have played and studied the game for 50 years or more, and still a thoughtful session on the practice tee will help you play a better—and therefore more satisfying—game the next time out.

The Learning Process

Before we begin taking up the means of improving your golf, I would like to say a few words about the learning process. Good golf is not easily learned. No doubt it would lose much of its appeal if it were.

Good style is not easily captured. Long and intelligent study and practice is the only means by which you can come to acquire a sound golf stroke. There will be many ups and downs along the path to lower scores. I cannot tell you how many times the game has deflated, even humiliated, me. The Scots called it "an 'umblin' game." They were so right.

In this connection, the one and only Robert T. Jones, Jr., the immortal Grand Slam Champion, tells this story on himself. "I was a very young man when I first played East Lake at Atlanta, my home course, in 63. After the round, I confided to my father that I had the game figured out, and didn't expect to go over 70 ever again. The very next time out I had to struggle to shoot 77." This is from the most heroic figure the game has produced.

The same type of thing undoubtedly will happen to you. One day you will find that you are, say, driving the ball exceptionally far and straight. You will be brought to think that at last you have the driving problem figured out. Then, the next time out your driving will be terrible, and maybe you will putt exceptionally well. You think to yourself that some fine day you will get them all together—the driving, the irons, the chipping, the putting, and all.

Probably you will. Then will come the strong temptation to think you have pretty well mastered the game. "I am improving," you will say, "and I shall continue to improve." You will be exultant. You will be proud. You will envision a long string of victories over your regular opponents (you are apt, in fact, to pity them a little). And— I really hate to say this—you will generally be wrong. You will be improving, right enough, but improvement in golf just never follows a straight upward path.

Do not despair when the poorer rounds come. Remember that the pleasure lies in conquering the tough problems. Stay with it. You will begin again to improve. And this time (maybe) you will remember not to be too exultant, too proud. Then you will REALLY be learning the game.

This book is written in the earnest belief that it will help the reader play better (and hence more enjoyable) golf. There are those who say that the game cannot be learned from books. I disagree.

I know from talking to golfers of varying degrees of ability that many of them fail to understand even the fundamentals of the golf swing. I have often heard golfers of advanced age and long experience announce with glee that they have just "discovered" something about the game. And their "discovery" is frequently something I had been considering as basic for a number of years. This sort of thing suggests to me a lot of golf problems stick around to plague us simply because we of the golf clan fail to tell each other what we know.

This book contains what I know.

CARY MIDDLECOFF'S
MASTER
GUIDE
TO
GOLF

A

ADDRESS TO THE BALL: When taking your position at address, consider the ball in relation to an imaginary line midway between your heels and at right angles to the line to your target. The position of the ball on either side of this dividing line is all-important to your game.

One of your principal aims in golf is to make your swing as consistent as possible. This achievement is often referred to as "grooving the swing." The clubs vary in length, and your swing varies according to the club you're using. The woods require a more sweeping stroke, while the swing with the irons is a downward blow. Therefore, in order to keep your stroke consistent, you must position the ball before each stroke to fit both club length and swing.

If the ball remained in a constant position, you would have to make the proper adjustments by changing your hand action. This

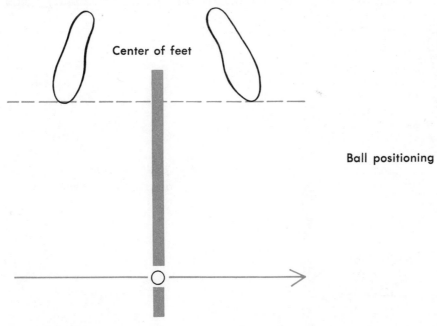

Center of feet

Ball positioning

would be especially difficult for the player who doesn't play or practice constantly. It's easier and more effective to change the position of the ball.

POSITION OF THE BALL FOR WOODS

For the driver, the ball should be positioned approximately even with the right instep. I say "approximately" because the individual player may want to alter the position a bit in accordance with his build and swing—in fact, very often he should. The majority of better players play the ball off the left instep—the result of considerable thought and experimentation.

The proper positioning spot for the fairway woods (the 2, 3, and 4) is back about one turn of the ball, say an inch. That's because you hit these shots with more of a down-and-through swing than you do with the driver. Also, these clubs are slightly shorter than the driver, which means that you reach the bottom of the swing arc a fraction sooner. But since the differences in clubs are very slight, the changes in ball positioning should be slight too.

Play the fairway woods from a spot even with the left heel when the lie is reasonably good. If the lie is fairly close, move the ball back just a fraction toward the right foot, as you would (or should) when

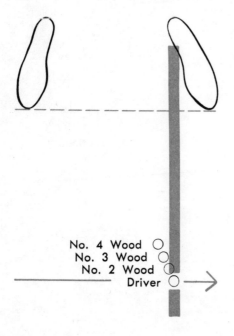

Ball positioning for woods
in relation to driver

No. 4 Wood ○
No. 3 Wood ○
No. 2 Wood ○
Driver ○ →

hitting a more down-and-through blow to raise the ball. Should you position the ball still more toward center if the lie is very close? No, then you use an iron.

POSITION OF THE BALL FOR IRONS

For a 2-iron shot, the ball should be positioned just to the right (or inside) of the left heel. With the 3-iron, the position is about a half turn of the ball nearer the center of the feet. The 4, 5 and 6-irons are played very near the center of the feet. The 5-iron is played directly in the center—the key position for these three clubs. Play the 4-iron just barely ahead of center, the 6-iron barely behind.

The position for the 7, 8 and 9-irons is slightly behind center. Note that the stance becomes narrower as the club lengths decrease, so that even for the 9-iron shot the ball rests no more than an inch behind center. For a full shot play the pitching wedge from the same spot as the 9-iron.

The changes in positioning for various shots are very slight but nonetheless important. If you are afflicted with general wildness— that is, missing indiscriminately on the right and left—you are probably placing the ball carelessly at address (*see* SPRAYING).

When you position the ball for a sand trap shot, you place it as you

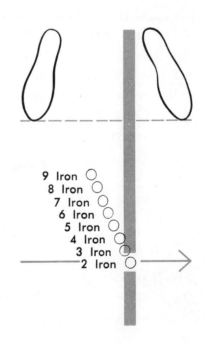

Ball positioning for irons in
relation to No. 2 Iron

9 Iron
8 Iron
7 Iron
6 Iron
5 Iron
4 Iron
3 Iron
2 Iron

would for the driver. Because you must use a different stroke when playing from sand traps, the placement requires special attention, which is fully explained under SAND TRAPS. Also see the special address to the ball for putts, described under PUTTING.

The position of the ball at address is prescribed in more detail with the treatment of each club under CLUBS and PUTTING.

APPROACH PUTT: *See* PUTTING

APPROACH TO THE BALL: The approach to the ball (the series of movements prior to assuming your stance) must be considered a part of the swing. In this brief preliminary action—and it should be brief—the success or failure of a given shot is often determined.

These pre-stance movements should set up a rhythmic pattern for the waggle and the swing. Imagine that you're about to step onto the dance floor with a partner: you pick up the beat of the music even before you begin dancing. The same preparation goes into the golf swing. This isn't to suggest that you go into a ritual dance before you step up to hit a golf shot! But you should prepare yourself mentally and physically before you take your stance.

My method is to plant my right foot first, recheck the line of the shot and then step in smoothly with the left foot to set my stance. If I feel then that I haven't done it right, I step back with my left foot and get set again. You may prefer a different method; but, whatever approach technique you adopt, you will make a better swing if you follow some rhythmic pattern in stepping up to the ball and get yourself set to time the swing properly (*see* BACKSWING, DOWNSWING *and* SWING [GENERAL]).

B

BACKSWING: Let's consider the backswing as a complete unit before we examine its parts. For simplicity's sake, I'd like to discusss the backswing for the full drive. The same principles apply to the back-swings for the other clubs (excluding the sand wedge, which is taken up under SAND TRAPS). The only difference between the driver back-swing and the others is that it calls for the maximum pivot, weight exchange, length of arc and left heel action (lifting the left heel). These actions are more restricted in the normal swings for the other clubs because the clubs themselves are shorter.

I deal with these slight changes in the treatment of each club under CLUBS.

PURPOSE

The purpose of the backswing is: (1) to get the hands in the proper position to deliver the blow and the body in the right position to assist the hands (by not interfering with them) and (2) to set up the proper timing (or rhythm) for the swing.

SPEED

The backswing must be smooth and unhurried. Most players tend to rush it, though a few players are too slow.

The most important thing to remember about backswing speed is that you must swing the club back fast enough to maintain your timing yet slow enough to give yourself the feel of a smooth, unhurried action.

If your backswing is too fast or too slow, you'll lose your balance near the top of the swing. When too fast, the backswing will pull or jerk you off balance because you must stay too long in positions in which your weight is not centered.

It's not necessarily true that some persons should swing back faster than others by virtue of individual habits and temperament. A person who is naturally quick will swing faster than a person who does things slowly and deliberately. But there are limits in both cases.

Comparisons of timing between the backswings and downswings of the best players show that the backswing moves at about one-third the speed of the downswing. This one-to-three ratio should work for all of us.

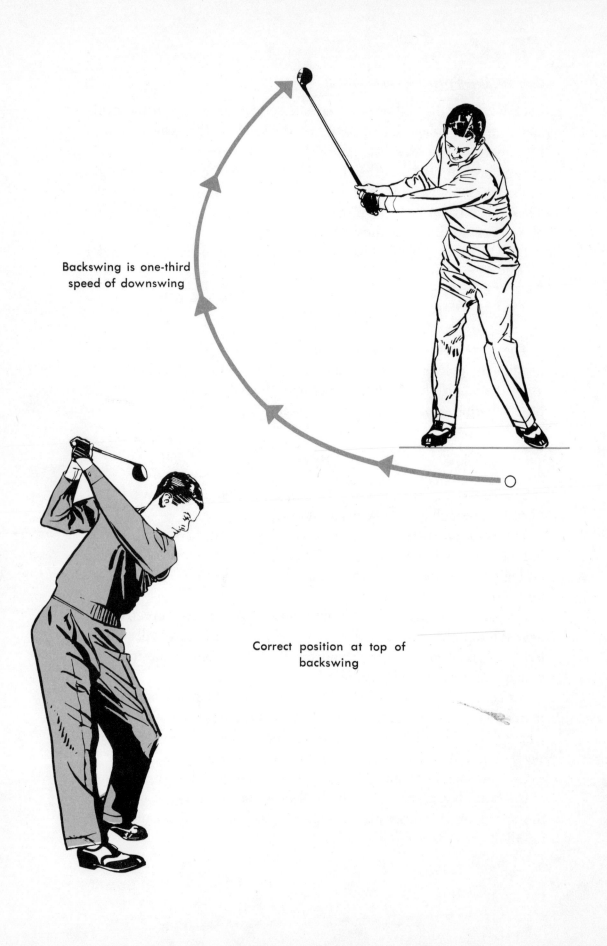

Backswing is one-third
speed of downswing

Correct position at top of
backswing

BODY POSITION

At the top of the backswing your body should be coiled to strike. Your hips and shoulders are turned, your hands cocked and your right elbow pointing to the ground and close to the body. Your weight is on your right side, your knees are still flexed as they were at address, your left arm is straight and your left knee and ankle are turned in with the heel slightly off the ground (remember that this is the driver backswing). **And your head is still in the same position as it was at the beginning of the swing.**

LENGTH

The length of the backswing also varies to some extent according to the individual. Supple golfers naturally swing back further than

Club should go no further than parallel with ground

compact, heavily muscled players. But again there are limits to be observed.

At the top of my driver backswing the shaft is almost but not quite parallel to the ground: *i.e.*, the plane from my hands to the clubhead is slightly upward. Some good players reach the top of the swing with the club pointing slightly downward. I maintain that the club should remain parallel with the ground.

What you wish to achieve is a happy medium (golf calls for many happy mediums). You want a **full** backswing for maximum power. But you also want a **controlled** backswing for accuracy and consistency.

If you can do so without straining, lift the club (driver) back to the point where its shaft is parallel to the ground and pointing along the line of flight—but no further. Failing that, swing it back as far as you can without straining. That will be your full backswing.

One great danger of the overlength backswing is that it forces you to partially release the club with the left hand (the piccolo grip), and this affects your accuracy even more than your power.

One danger of the too long backswing is the "Piccolo Grip"

FIRST BACKSWING MOVEMENT (FORWARD PRESS)

Paradoxically, the first movement of the backswing is a slight forward motion of the entire swinging mechanism—hands, arms and body. In recent years, this little action has come to be known as the forward press, though good players have been doing it for decades.

Its purpose is to impart to the backswing a smooth, fluid start. You make the little forward movement and then return smoothly past the

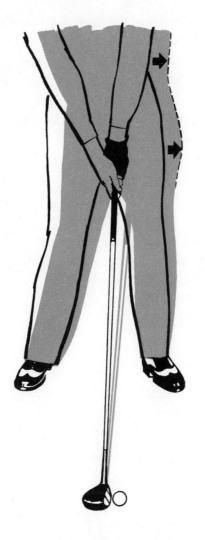

The Forward Press

original starting point. This prevents any abruptness of movement in taking the club away from the ball.

Some players who use the forward press for the first time tend to overdo it. Remember that the movement is very slight and barely perceptible. Your hands move forward about an inch; you turn your body likewise.

TAKEAWAY

Following the forward press and recoil, we are now into what is called the takeaway: the first 12 to 18 inches of the backswing.

Remember that you swing the club straight back from the ball, keeping it low along the ground to insure a wide arc, while the club-face remains square to the line of flight until the movement is complete. Also, you don't turn your body until near the end of the take-away. You can take the club back a few inches without turning your body; don't turn until you have to, so that the action will be smooth and natural.

Keep your hands away from your body as you take back the club. Many players pull their hands in close to the body as they begin the takeaway. With a backswing that's too much inside you're likely to use a wide hook.

In actual play, it is wise to pick out a spot eight to ten inches straight behind the ball where the clubhead will pass low along the ground and square to the target. You can train yourself in practice by sticking a tee in the ground eight to ten inches behind the ball and knocking it over as you take back the club.

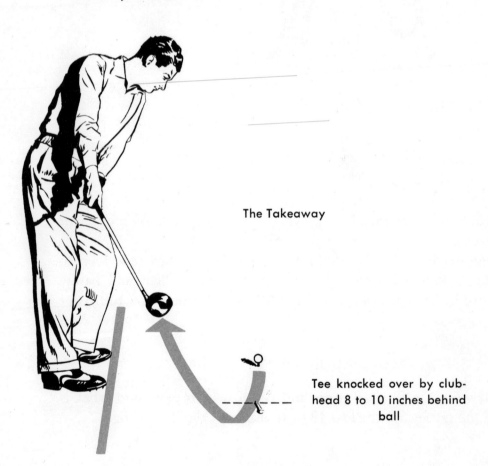

The Takeaway

Tee knocked over by club-head 8 to 10 inches behind ball

The Takeaway should be
smooth, slow and low

That is the phase of the backswing known as the takeaway. It should be smooth and slow, low along the ground and straight away from the ball. But the takeaway is only a phase of the backswing and should not be considered as a separate movement. In this discussion we dissect the backswing in order to look at its various parts separately. Nevertheless, we must not forget that the backswing—indeed, the entire swing—is a one-piece affair whose primary objective is simplicity.

There may be times when you locate some particular fault in taking the club away from the ball. That's why I want you to be able to look at the foregoing to find the correct answer.

WEIGHT SHIFT

When addressing a full shot, your weight is evenly divided between both feet. The forward press puts a little extra weight on the right foot, but that is incidental. As the recoil from the forward press begins, your body and hands are back even with the ball and your weight is again evenly distributed.

At this point you slowly and gradually shift your weight to the left foot for the backswing. At the end of the takeaway the weight shift will have been very slight. Then it becomes more rapid, though always smooth and gradual.

At the top of the full drive backswing, about 80 per cent of your weight should be on the right foot. Don't worry about exceeding that amount. You can tell whether you have made a proper weight shift when you feel that you are in a balanced position to deliver a blow of maximum power.

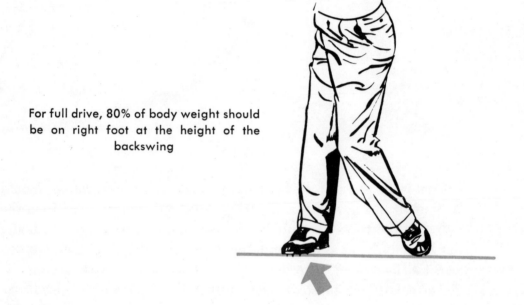

For full drive, 80% of body weight should be on right foot at the height of the backswing

LEFT HEEL, ANKLE AND KNEE ACTION

Unless you are very supple and/or have a very short backswing, you will find it necessary to raise the left heel off the ground to reach the top position you want for a full stroke. But don't raise the left heel more than is necessary.

When you begin to shift your weight and coil your body on the backswing, your left leg must yield when the left knee and ankle turn in.

This inward turning of the ankle and knee will give you all the leeway you need for 6-iron and shorter shots. For a 5-iron shot, the

Inward turning of left knee and ankle for No. 6 Iron, with left heel remaining on ground

left heel will barely clear the ground. You'll raise it more for the longer shots (two inches for the driver).

Remember that raising the left heel is not an end in itself. Actually, the left heel is "pulled" off the ground in the final stage of the backswing. In actual play you should not be aware of your left heel action. But in setting up or correcting your swing, you need only realize that the left heel should come off the ground only enough to permit a full, free backswing.

You keep the lift at a minimum so that the left heel is replaced at the exact moment the downswing begins. So, the less you raise it, the more easily you can set it down. If the left heel is not replaced just so, accuracy is impossible. A half inch off may easily make a difference of ten to twenty yards in the line of flight.

If you raise the left heel too high, you're likely to sway laterally to the right on the backswing. This changes the position of your head, and only trouble can result.

Remember that the first action is an inward turn of the left ankle and knee. Of course, the ankle will only turn in slightly. The left knee should turn in three or four inches on a full shot. When these actions

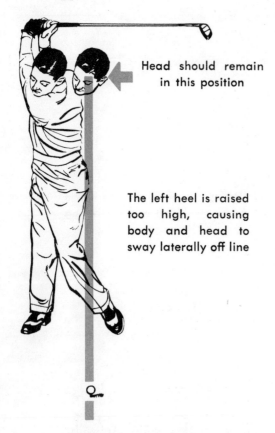

Head should remain in this position

The left heel is raised too high, causing body and head to sway laterally off line

Body turn inside barrel

fail to give you sufficient body rotation, let the left heel come off the ground.

There are a few good players who hit every shot without ever raising the left heel. A number of others have experimented with this method and discarded it. The best opinion definitely favors raising the left heel to the extent necessary to achieve a full backswing with complete freedom of movement—and no more.

HIP TURN

The hips must turn or swivel on the backswing in order to place the body in a powerful hitting position. Also, you must get the right hip out of the way of the right elbow to permit free passage of the arms and hands as they come through on the downswing.

The hip turning action is a rotation around a stationary axis. There must be no lateral sway accompanying the turn, since this makes your head move. Of course, you might recover from a lateral sway and hit the ball straight, but it could only happen now and then.

Some professionals say that you think of yourself as standing inside a barrel when you swing. I recommend this suggestion. Turn the hips, but avoid moving them laterally.

SHOULDER TURN

In the backswing, the shoulders turn enough so that you can bring your hands into the proper hitting position at the top of the swing.

You begin the swing with the right shoulder about two inches below the left because the right hand must drop below the left to grip the club. At the top of the backswing the left shoulder will be about two inches below the right.

In the course of the backswing, your shoulders will not quite make a half turn. At address, the left shoulder will be pointing about 10 degrees left of your objective, and at the top of the full backswing your shoulders will be turned so that the left shoulder is pointing at right angles to the ball and the intended line of flight.

At address the left shoulder points 10° to left of objective

At top of backswing the left shoulder points at right angles to the objective

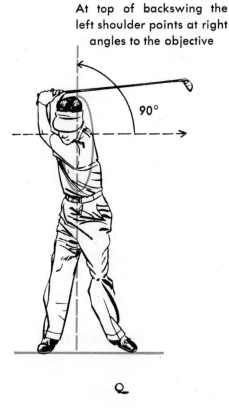

ACTION AT TOP OF BACKSWING
(TO PAUSE OR NOT TO PAUSE)

Many top professionals and golf theorists disagree as to whether or not you should pause at the top of the backswing. I pause for about a full count, because this slight hesitation helps my timing on the downswing and enables me to check my aim and position. I feel sure that if I paused at the top for more than one count (a fraction of a second), it would disrupt my timing. And I have no doubt that even the slight pause I use would disrupt the timing of some players. Thus the problem is really an individual one.

I play a lot of golf and practice a lot, and I have used the pause for a long time now. So I can time the swing to include the pause. A person who plays and practices less than I do may not be able to do this.

You mustn't think of the pause as a separate step apart from the swing as a whole. The action at the top must be smooth and unhurried. The pause might be classed as just an exaggeration of taking your time at the top of the backswing. Never be in a hurry to go from backswing to downswing. Remember that the backswing must come to a stop, however brief, before the downswing is begun.

STRAIGHT LEFT ARM

"Keep the left arm straight," says the old golf admonition, and it's as sound a piece of advice as it ever was. In the proper address position, the left arm should be straight, forming a straight line with the shaft from the shoulder to the ball. It is only logical then that the left arm should remain straight throughout the backswing until the ball is hit, since you must bring the club back to the ball in the initial position.

The only trouble here is that many players—beginners especially—confuse the straight left arm with a rigid arm with the elbow joint locked. Many players find it physically impossible to reach a full backswing position with a straight left arm, but they still manage to play good golf.

Keep the left arm as straight as you can, but don't feel that this is essential for hitting the ball correctly.

Correct—Straight left arm
at top of the backswing

Incorrect—Left arm is too
rigid

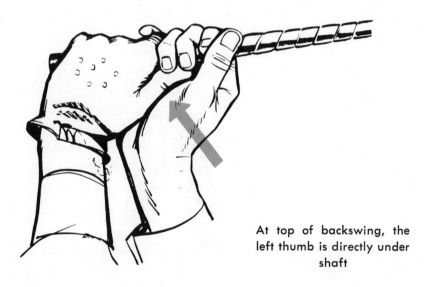

At top of backswing, the
left thumb is directly under
shaft

HANDS AT THE TOP

If you want to picture how the hands should look at the top of the swing, think of the left thumb as being directly under the shaft. In this position, the palms will be directly opposite each other as they were at address.

Don't consciously cock your wrists on the backswing. This action is automatic, and you may be sure it has been properly carried out if the right thumb is under the shaft at the top. No other check is necessary.

As for the placement of the hands at the top, they should be just slightly (an inch or two) behind the line of the shoulders. This is your power position, which allows for the full hip turn necessary for a full-power blow.

Your grip on the club must be firm; you can't let go in either hand. You must avoid a tendency to loosen your grip with the last three fingers of the left hand. This can ruin your shot. (The point, taken up more fully under GRIP, is important enough to bear repeating.)

Placement of the hands at the top is slightly behind the right shoulder

Too fast backswing pulling player off balance

COMMON BACKSWING FAULTS

Backswing too fast: If you are an average golfer, you've doubtless been told countless times that your backswing is too fast. And it probably is. It's one of the average golfer's most common faults.

To repeat, the two main purposes of the backswing are: (1) to place your hands and body (particularly your hands) in the proper hitting position and (2) to initiate the correct rhythm or timing for the swing. The second point applies to the speed of your backswing.

Backswing speed varies with the individual to some extent. The player who is naturally brisk and fast should swing the club back faster than the more deliberate golfer. Some persons do things best at a fast pace; others are profitably slow. Thus, although the proper backswing speed is different for each player, it is not too fast for either.

We're all anxious to make the shot and watch the ball on its way toward the flag. If the shot is a tough one, our anxiety is such that we unconsciously speed up the swing—just when we should slow it down.

If your backswing is too hasty, try to imagine it in advance as a smooth, unhurried action. Once you get in the habit of thinking about this action, you'll be in the right frame of mind to tackle a tough situation.

Let me repeat: proper backswing speed varies to some extent with the individual, making it impossible to prescribe a single speed that will work for all. Recently, however, a study of backswing speeds was made among the leading professionals, and they proved to be roughly a third of the downswing speed for both short shots and full drives. The results of this test provide a sound basis for gauging your own backswing speed.

The backswing that moves too quickly can cause a lot of woe. In the first place, the very essence of good timing depends on your ability to sense the position and action of your hands and clubhead throughout the swing. This is impossible if you rush the swing. Also, it's difficult to stop an overzealous backswing and then begin the downswing without being pulled off balance.

The fast backswing defeats its own purpose. You can only achieve maximum power if the initial actions of your swing are slow and smooth, building up to maximum speed at impact. When you're too fast with your backswing, the clubhead speed diminishes by the time you hit the ball.

Backswing too slow: When your backswing is too slow—a rare but potent fault—you'll also disrupt your timing. The slow backswing can be a valuable asset but only to a point. Players who slow this part of the swing to a snail's pace do so on bad advice or because of a too literal approach to golf.

But what do we mean by "too slow"? "Unnaturally slow" would be the best answer. Remember that you are trying to achieve a well-timed swing that builds up gradually in speed and power. When you take back the club haltingly and then speed up your action abruptly on the downswing, your timing must suffer.

Then too, you lose your balance at the top of the swing, which is never an easy position to maintain for any considerable length of time. Only a fluid total swing will preserve your balance.

Estimate the proper backswing speed as roughly a third the speed of your downswing. Better not make it much more—or less.

For further discussions of the backswing, see DOWNSWING, DRIVING, PUTTING and SWING (GENERAL).

BANK-CLIMBING SHOT: An overhanging limb or other intervening obstacle may force you to keep the ball low. Or a pin may be set so close to the side of the green nearest you that you can't get in close with a pitch shot. Try the bank-climbing run-up shot when the lie is too close for pitch lofting.

The bank climbing Run-up
  Shot with a 2 Iron

You hit the ball low along the ground with such force that it climbs up the bank of the green and dies shortly thereafter. Try to keep the shot *low*. A shot that produces a series of low bounces at the base of the bank will give you better control. A high bounce, you see, may get *into* the bank and stop, or the ball may clear the bank of the green on the big hop and go all the way over. (It's all but impossible to tell which it will do.)

The low bounces enable the ball to *climb*, though the intervening ground should be relatively clear: *i.e.*, no high grass to grab the ball, and no bunkers between your position and the bank of the green.

To execute the low shot, choose one of your less lofted irons. (A 2-iron is always a good choice.) Position the ball to the right of the imaginary line between your feet. A crisp downward blow straight through the ball is the stroke you want.

Quite often the putter, with face slightly opened for loft, will prove the most effective weapon. But aim slightly to the left of your objective to compensate for the right trend.

BELLYING: *See* LOW SHOTS

BLADING: *See* LOW SHOTS

BRASSIE: *See* CLUBS

BREAKING PUTTS: *See* PUTTING

BUMP SHOT: The bump shot is very similar to the bank-climber. Use it when circumstances rule out the lofted pitch.

On the bump shot you wing the ball into the bank of the green on a low line. But, unlike the climber, it should stay airborne until it hits the bank. Why? So the force of the shot will cause the ball to bounce up and *over* the bank. There should always be some forward slant to the bank of the green. Without it, you can't work the bump shot.

Again the ball must be kept *low*. Don't let it clear the bank of the green on the fly. If you do, you'll probably end up far away on the

The Bump Shot underneath the low-hanging branches of a tree over deep grass

other side. You want a low liner that bangs into the side of the green with plenty of momentum to carry it up and over.

When the terrain (high grass or the like) makes it necessary to keep the ball in the air all the way to the bank of the green, use the bump shot rather than the climber.

The execution is the same as for the climber, but you sock the ball harder. This is a chancy shot, sometimes a desperation shot—the one chance to reach the green. If you are forced to use it, give it everything you've got or you're sure to miss (*see* BANK-CLIMBING SHOT).

C

CASUAL WATER RULE: *See* WEATHER

CHIP SHOT: *See* SCORING RANGE

CLUBS: The chief objectives of this section are to give the player a better general understanding of his golf clubs and to provide a reference guide for players who may be having trouble with a particular club, or perhaps with a certain group of clubs, such as the middle irons.

There are a number of golfing types who, in my opinion, cost themselves strokes because the clubs they use are not those best suited for their particular games. The first of these to come to mind is the player who, through sentiment or a false sense of economy, keeps the same set of golf clubs year after year—perhaps the set with which he won some tournament or important match a dozen years ago. Maybe he feels he doesn't play enough or seriously enough to warrant the necessary expenditure for a new set.

By adopting such an attitude the player denies himself the benefit of the many and continuing advances made by manufacturers of golf clubs: better balance, wider hitting area, better grips, and even better appearance, since hitting a golf ball is actually easier with a club that looks like a good club. It is a proven fact that golf clubs are better made each year. Engineering knowledge and laboratory tests continue to produce new models that are superior to the old ones. The competition between manufacturers sees to that.

I am not advocating that you turn in your old set every time a new model comes out. But I recommend that you stay abreast of the trends in buying and owning clubs. Do not keep your clubs until they are outmoded—until the wood in your wood clubs has lost its power to send the ball on out there or until the grooves in your irons are worn down to such an extent that you can no longer get the proper accuracy or underspin on the ball.

At the opposite extreme, another type of player costs himself strokes by changing clubs so often that he never gets quite used to a particular set. This type will often keep some extra sets at home or in his club locker and is never quite sure which set he should be using on a particular day. (He gets the uneasy feeling after one or two missed shots that he should have in his bag the set he left home, and vice versa.)

This latter type is the same fellow who likes to carry two putters in his bag on the theory that if he finds himself putting badly with one, he can shift to the other. But the fact that he has two that are handy tends to make him unsure as to which he should use for a particular putt. If only one were available to him, he could give all his concentration to the matter of making the putt, instead of wondering which of two putters he should have in his hand at the moment.

Still another type of player loses strokes because he has the wrong fourteen clubs in his bag. Perhaps he is carrying a 1-iron and leaving out a 4-wood—or vice versa, though this is less frequent. It may be that he is carrying one wedge, either a pitching wedge or a sand wedge, when he should be carrying both. In some instances a player should leave his 2-iron out of the bag and replace it with a 5-wood. In rarer instances, the driver should be left out, in favor of some other club, and a 2-wood used off the tee.

These matters will be taken up as the clubs are discussed individually below. But let me urge here that all golfers restrict to fourteen the number of clubs used for any particular round of play. This is a rule of golf and should not be deviated from, regardless of the informality of the game you are in. Only for strict practice should you carry more than the allotted number.

SELECTION

The first thing you want to know about your clubs, collectively and individually, is whether they fit you. Happily, this problem is far more easily solved than was the case some years ago. Unless your build varies greatly from the norm, rest assured that there is a factory-made set of clubs suited to your needs. Sets are now matched. The reputable factories employ specialists to see that they are.

You need only visit the pro shop where you play and let the pro look you over. Show him how you swing (if he doesn't already know), and you will be quickly and accurately advised as to a proper set of clubs for *you*.

This information will come in handy when you discuss the clubs you should use with your professional. But here are some other points of general information that will also be helpful:

(1) If you are of medium build and strength and play on an average of twice a week or less, you should have clubs of medium weight with shafts of medium flexibility.

(2) If you play an average of three or four times a week or more, you should probably use heavier clubs with stiffer shafts, because the muscles you use for golf will be better developed than those of the average player.

(3) Regardless of how often you play, if you are an older person, you should probably use lighter-weight clubs with more flexible shafts.

(4) You may be of small or medium build; but, if your hands and wrists are especially well developed, as is often the case in certain lines of work, you should use heavier clubs with stiffer shafts.

(5) It is a good general rule that players with fast swings should use clubs with stiffer shafts, while slow swingers should use clubs with more flexible shafts.

(6) A "matched set" of golf clubs is a set in which the center of gravity in each club is located in the same relative position. In other words, the weight of the clubhead bears the same relation to the overall weight of the club. The idea of matched sets is to have all the clubs swing alike.

LENGTH

I would like to disabuse beginning golfers of one prevalent idea about golf club lengths. There is a belief, still widely held, that if a person is considerably taller than average, he needs clubs that are considerably longer than average. It ain't necessarily so.

If a person were considerably taller than average but had arms of average length, he would need clubs considerably longer than average. But the incidence of such cases is so small as to be negligible. With extremely rare exceptions, the tall person has long arms, the person of average height has arms of average length and the short person has short arms. Thus the three types mentioned will (or should) use clubs which do not vary greatly in length.

STANDARD WOODS

I would like to emphasize here that the differences in swing techniques among woods 1 through 4 are very slight. By experimenting with slightly different ball positions for each club, I've noticed that the swing becomes slightly more downward as one progresses from the 2-wood through to the 4. Occasionally, however, the 2, 3 and 4-wood swings are practically identical. Such instances occur when the distance to be covered is the main consideration, not the lie of the ball.

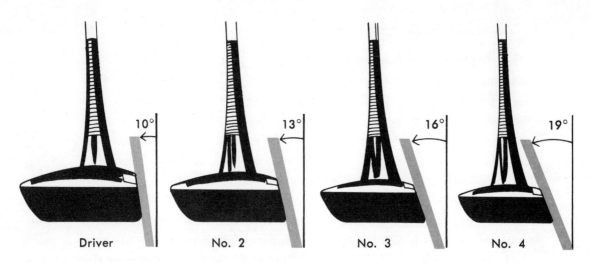

Degrees of loft for first 4 woods

When an excellent lie would permit you to use a 2-wood, though distance indicates a 4, you wouldn't have to hit down on the ball any more than you would with the 2. The swing would be almost a sweep.

Because of the many problems involved, I won't indicate the approximate distances to be expected for the various woods. There are long, short and medium hitters. Also, weather and course conditions vary greatly.

You should expect your distance to vary about ten yards per club with the woods, starting with the driver and ending with the 4-wood. If your average good drive is, say, 240 yards, you should expect about 230 with the 2-wood, 220 with the 3 and 210 with the 4. This is assuming that the ball is in a satisfactory lie for each club.

Remember that these four wood clubs are designed for distance. This does not mean that you shouldn't try to be as accurate with them as you possibly can. But you can't expect pinpoint accuracy with them.

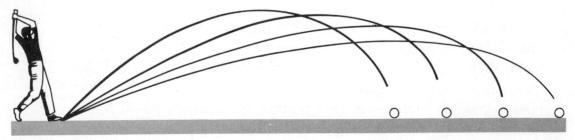

Approximate distance for standard woods

	No. 4	No. 3	No. 2	Driver
	210 yds.	220 yds.	230 yds.	240 yds.

If you need a wood club to reach the green and there's a heavy penalty for being slightly off line, you should give some thought to another line of play: *i.e.*, playing safe with an iron and hoping to get the next shot up for one putt. In other words, use your woods intelligently.

For the 1-wood or driver see DRIVER.

2-wood or brassie: Your 2-wood should be looked on primarily as a club to give you maximum distance off the fairway and put you in a favorable position for the succeeding shot. Its relative importance in your set will depend on the type of player you are. If you are short but accurate, usually hitting the fairway from the tee, you will likely use your 2-wood up to a dozen times during an average round. Long drivers, and especially those with a tendency to wildness, will play many rounds without using the 2-wood at all.

Selection of your 2-wood will hardly be a problem. It will usually be one of the matched set of woods you chose on the basis of the driver. If the 2-wood is not a part of a matched set, it should still be identical with the driver as to length and swing weight. It should be the same length as your driver even though the arc of the driver swing is slightly longer. The driver shots will be teed up, you see, bringing the ball a little nearer your hands. The 2-wood swing is slightly more downward in character so that the bottom of the arc is reached a little earlier in the swing. The differences offset each other.

2-wood swing: The differences between the 2-wood swing and the driver swing are minute. As mentioned above, the swing is just slightly downward in character—the perfect sweep that characterizes the driver. You should hit slightly down on the 2-wood shot in order to get it up. You want the ball to go up the face of the 2-wood, which has a loft of 13 degrees, 3 degrees more than the standard driver.

The one other slight change from the driver swing is in the positioning of the ball. But, as I've stated, the change is minute: the positioning is about half a turn of the ball nearer the center of the feet. Make the positioning just inside the left heel, because the bottom of the swing arc is reached a trifle earlier.

Aside from these minor differences, swing with the 2-wood as you would with the driver: full body turn, wide arc, left heel off the

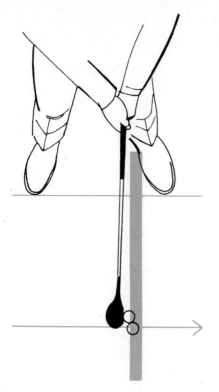

Ball position for No. 2 Wood

ground as needed for a full backswing, slow start on the downswing, full controlled power, full follow through and finish.

2-wood strategy: You should use the 2-wood *only* when the lie and the shot situation call for it.

If the 2-wood is to be your choice, the lie should be excellent: *i.e.,* the ball should be sitting up nicely on the grass, permitting you to get all of the clubface on it with a swing that is very nearly a perfect sweep. If there is any doubt about your chances of getting the ball up nicely and away with the 2-wood, you should choose a more lofted wood, which will give you better distance from a close or doubtful lie. Also, in a doubtful situation you are far less apt to dribble the ball along the ground.

As for the shot situation, many players feel constrained to use the 2-wood whenever there is a possible chance of reaching the green with that club. This should not be the criterion. There are times when a perfect brassie shot might put you on the green. But anything other than a perfect shot would leave you in a very poor position for the next try; whereas a shot played deliberately short with a more lofted wood or a long iron would be reasonably certain to leave you a simple chip or pitch for the next shot. In such a situation—which is not infrequent—the better strategy is to play short, even though there is a possibility of reaching the putting surface with the 2-wood.

Perfect brassie shots are fairly rare even with the best golfers. On the other hand, good chips or pitches of the type that make a one-putt green possible are within the capabilities of most golfers. So why risk all on a chance that is not very likely to come off? Isn't it much more sensible to risk the simpler shot—the chip or pitch? Here's a sample situation:

Situation: The seventh hole at the Medinah Country Club outside Chicago is a rather long par-five; but the last half of the hole is mostly downhill, making it possible for fairly long hitters to reach the green in two. The fairway becomes quite narrow as the green is approached; there are trees lining each side and the green itself is heavily trapped. You have a long drive, and a full brassie *might* put you on the green. However, if it is even slightly off line, you are apt to land in plenty of trouble.

Solution: This is no place to take a long chance with a 2-wood. Depend on the third shot and insure your chance of having a fairly simple third. Sacrifice distance. Play the ball short.

3-wood (spoon): The differences between the 2 and 3-wood are small. The standard face loft is 3 degrees greater (16 degrees). The shaft length is about an inch shorter (41½ to 42 inches standard). The lie is just a tiny bit more upright.

As with the 2-wood, selection of the 3-wood should offer no problem. It should belong to the driver and 2-wood set or, failing that, should be of the same swing weight.

3-wood swing: The swing with the 3-wood is no different from the 2-wood swing. It requires merely minor adjustment. The downswing is only slightly more downward in character, so that you reach the bottom of the swing arc a little earlier. That's why the club is slightly shorter and its lie a little more upright. But note that the differences are minute.

In line with the slightly more downward blow and upright lie of the club itself, there is the necessity for a slight adjustment in the positioning of the ball at address. Naturally, it goes a bit nearer the center of the feet. Play it off the left heel.

3-wood strategy: On most golf courses you will have more bona fide occasions to use the 3-wood than the 2. This is because the 3-wood is effective from an average fairway lie and can also be used from the better lies in rough that is not too deep. And it follows that you will get more lies of this type than the exceptional ones that call for the 2-wood.

As an example of the proper use of the 3-wood, let's go back to the 13th hole at the Augusta National:

Situation: After a 230-yard drive slightly to the right of center of the fairway, the ball is in an average fairway lie and about 240 yards short of the creek that runs in front of the green.

Solution: The 3-wood would seem to fit all the specifications for this shot. You should have no difficulty in getting the ball up from a normal fairway lie with the 3-wood. The distance to be covered before reaching the creek, 240 yards, figures to be more than can normally be expected from a 3-wood, which would leave the ball safely short of the creek for an easy pitch to the green on the third.

Note that even a very short hitter would be foolish to take a 2-wood for this shot. Lacking an exceptionally good lie, he may very well fail to get the ball up and end up with a shot that's too long to reach the green on his third.

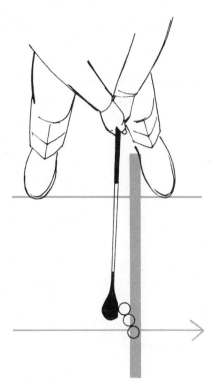

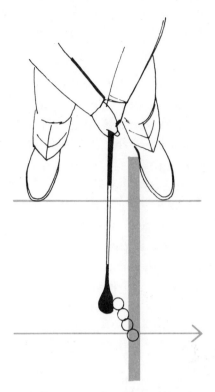

Ball position for No. 3 Wood   Ball position for No. 4 Wood

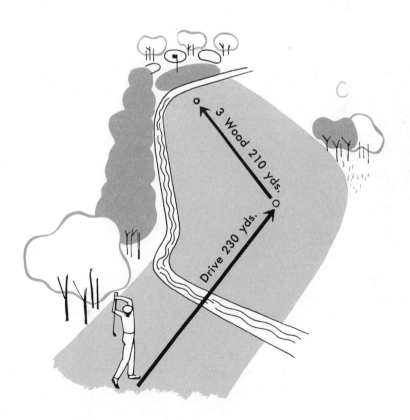

4-wood: The 4-wood is a very handy club. With its 3 degrees more loft than the 3-wood (19 degrees), it is excellent for shots from close lies in the fairway and can be used with good effect from fair lies in the rough. It is also a great aid in bridging the gap in distance between the 3-wood and 2-iron. The standard 4-wood has a shaft length of 41 inches, a half inch shorter than the 3-wood, and the standard lie is just under 56 degrees, which makes the club slightly more upright than the 3.

4-wood swing: The only difference between the 4 and the 3-wood swing is that the 4 is usually a little more downward in character, though this difference is extremely slight. The ball positioning is almost the same. Position the ball barely inside the left heel or a fraction of an inch nearer the center of the feet than you would for the 3-wood.

4-wood strategy: The 4-wood should be used for maximum distance when the lie is a little too close or deep to make the 3 a safe choice.

The No. 4 Wood should be used when the lie is a little too deep for a 3 Wood

As for distance, the 4-wood will yield about ten yards less than the 3 for the average player. From comparable lies, the 4-wood figures to give a little more height than the 3, coupled with slightly less roll.

DEEPER WOODS

The 6 and 7-woods are of even more recent origin than the 5, and I have seen a number of players with woods more lofted than these that were made to order and marked with higher numbers.

I have separated these clubs from the standard woods since they overlap the long irons for distance. Distance-wise, the 4-wood and 1-iron also overlap. But the 4-wood has become much more a part of the standard set than the 1-iron, which is used almost exclusively by the experts.

Without doubt, many players can benefit by using these deeper woods in place of the long irons. This is especially true of the 5-wood as a substitute for the 2-iron. Many golfers, especially those of less than average ability, find the 2-iron a difficult club to handle. They can't get the ball up consistently with this long iron. On the other hand, the 5-wood, which is only a degree more lofted in the face than the 2-iron, is an easy club for lifting.

To a lesser degree, the same relationship holds for the 6-wood and 3-iron, etc.

As I see it, the use of these deeper woods in place of the long irons is the compromise we make with the game of golf. In other words, it's easier to make *fair* shots with the deeper woods than the irons because they have a larger hitting area on the clubface. But the golfer who strives and masters the long irons will be the better player for it in the long run. Assuming that the shot is hit correctly, the irons are simply better implements for getting the ball close to the hole.

The superiority of the long irons over the deeper woods is even more pronounced when wind influences the play. A 6-wood might be fine on a still day or in a following wind, but using it to play the ball into a stiff wind poses the very tough problem of too much loft.

It might be argued then that the wise course is to own both the deeper woods and the long irons, using the latter only on windy days. Yet how could you hope to become adept with both?

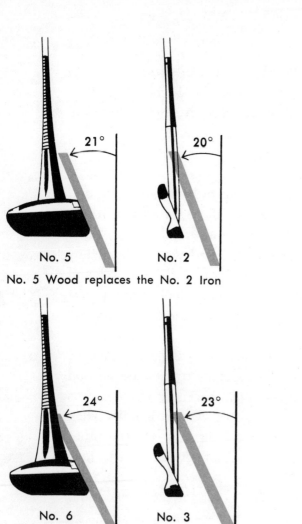

No. 5 Wood replaces the No. 2 Iron

No. 6 Wood replaces the No. 3 Iron

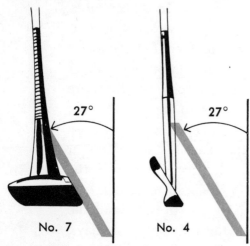

No. 7 Wood replaces the No. 4 Iron

The iron swing is a downward swing

I would use the deeper woods in place of long irons if you have been playing for a number of years and have a type of swing that prevents you from gaining the height you need with the long irons. But if you are dead set on making good with the long irons, stick with 'em.

The swing for the deeper woods should be the same as for the 4 wood with the ball positioned just slightly nearer the center of the feet.

IRONS (GENERAL)

The irons are the weapons with which you must really attack the course if you are to score well. The swing is down and through the ball, and you must trust in the loft of the clubface to give it the required lift. Never try to "pick the ball up" with your hands.

The irons fall into three general categories—long, medium and short. The 1 iron (should you be one of the few who carry it) and the 2 and 3-irons are regarded as the long irons. The 4, 5 and 6-irons rate as medium irons. That leaves the 7, 8, 9 and the pitching wedge as the short irons.

With the long irons you should generally aim for the biggest part of the green so that you'll have the widest possible margin for error while still trying to hit the green. The best strategy for the medium irons is likewise to aim for the middle of the green rather than the hole where the pin is tucked away in a corner. Here the margin for error may be reduced to some extent. With the short irons you should definitely be on the attack—you should go for the pin unless the scoring situation demands caution.

Iron sets are so designed that the average golfer will normally note a difference of about ten yards in range. You should take this into account in your choice of weapons. If you are not certain that you can reach the target with, say, a 5-iron, check to see whether overshooting by thirty feet or less will hurt you. If not, resolve the doubt in favor of the longer club, the 4-iron.

Underclubbing costs the golfing population more strokes a day than you could shake a stick at—a golf club, that is.

Remember that the iron you choose should be one with which you can reach the hole *comfortably*. Far too many golfers base their

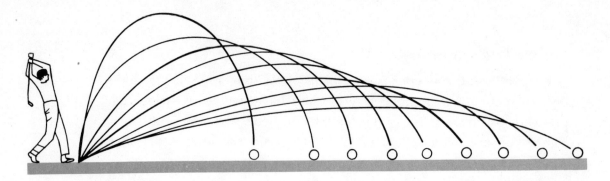

Pitching Wedge No. 9 No. 8 No. 7 No. 6 No. 5 No. 4 No. 3 No. 2 Iron
90 yds.   110   120   135   145   155   170   185   200 yds.

Approximate distance for irons

choice of irons on a different concept. They pick out the most lofted club in order to reach the green. To repeat, you should choose an iron that will allow you to reach your objective comfortably.

LONG IRONS

For the average-length hitter, long irons cover distances from 170 to 200 yards into the green. This is an extremely important range because it includes many second shots on par-four holes of average length and over, as well as a lot of par-three hole tee-shots.

If you are bent on improving your golf, start with the long irons, which can spell the difference between a good golfer and a fair one. Practice with the long irons, and you'll begin to lower your scores. Many players don't practice with these irons because they're somewhat afraid of them.

Long-iron practice will help you with the other irons. See for yourself. You'll notice that a golfer who plays his 2 and 3-irons well does equal credit to the rest of the irons. The opposite is not necessarily true. You will often see golfers who play their irons confidently and effectively *after* they reach the 4-iron range and under.

1-iron: This once standard club has in recent years all but vanished from the golfing scene. With the advent of the 4-wood back in the 1930's, the 1-iron began to lose some of its popularity, and when the United States Golf Association passed its rule that no more than fourteen clubs could be carried for a single round, most manufacturers no longer included the 1-iron in their standard sets.

For one thing, the two clubs hit for similar distances. With no wind, the 4-wood and the 1-iron go for equal distance on a solid shot. The 1-iron is perhaps a bit stronger against the wind because its shots describe a lower trajectory. But the 4-wood is stronger with the wind on the strength of the higher trajectory that follows.

However, the average golfer has discarded the 1-iron because it's difficult to use. You've got to hit the ball almost dead center on the clubface to produce a good shot. The face of the 1-iron offers only a small area for hitting shots of maximum distance. But if the ball is hit somewhat in the toe or heel with the 4-wood, it may travel fairly well due to the large clubface area, nearly twice that of the 1-iron.

Comparison of No. 4 Wood and No. 1 Iron, showing larger hitting area on the No. 4 Wood

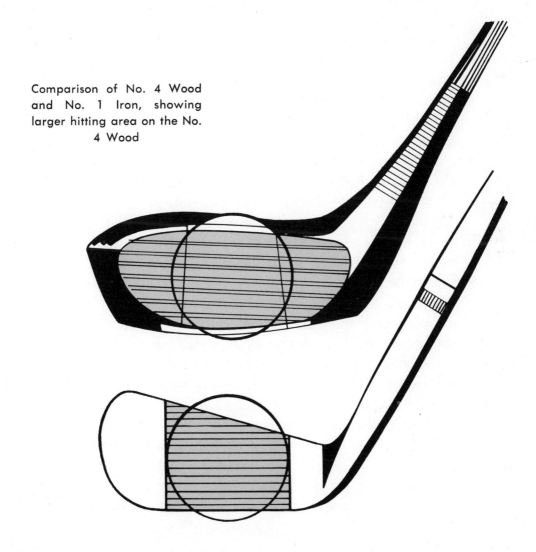

Also, the average golfer shies away from the 1-iron because the club *looks* hard to use effectively. The fact is that it looks harder than it actually is.

The 1-iron has a loft of 18 degrees, which is two more than the standard 3-wood and only two degrees less than the 2-iron. In shaft length and lie, it is virtually identical with the 2-iron. These comparisons show that the club has plenty of loft for raising the ball. You have only to hit down and through it.

1-iron swing: Despite the relatively rare use of the 1-iron, I want to describe the swing in some detail. The lessons to be learned apply to all the irons, particularly to the 2 and 3-irons.

The basic difference between the swing for the irons and the woods is that the former is a more pronounced down-and-through swing. We have seen that the swing for the driver is a sweep—you hit the ball just as the clubhead reaches the end of the swing arc and starts upward. While slightly downward in character, the swing with the other woods is more of a near sweep. As far as the irons are concerned, beginning with the 1-iron, the action is a definite *sweep,* not a down-and-through stroke.

As for ball position at address, we have seen that the changes for the various wood clubs are very slight, ranging from the left instep (for the driver) to the left heel (for the 4-wood). Assuming that the left foot is turned out at the prescribed 30 degrees, two inches would cover the entire range. For the 1-iron, the position of the ball at address should be about an inch inside the left heel—*i.e.,* an inch nearer the center of the feet. This represents a small but *definite* shift of the ball nearer the center of the feet. Since the down-and-through stroke becomes more pronounced as you start on the irons, you'll reach the bottom of the arc earlier in the swing.

The differences in the iron and wood swings are small. But they are clear and definite. You are looking for a *crisp* as well as a *solid* hit with the irons.

Here are the main differences:

(*1*) You should swing the irons back in a straight line away from the ball and in a fairly wide arc, but you cut down slightly on the arc and pick up the club a little more abruptly on the *takeaway.* If you think about it, you will see that this slight change is only logical:

if the downswing is slightly more downward in character, it follows that the backswing should move upward a little more.

(2) Your body rotation is a little more restricted than it is in the wood swing. This figures since you are swinging crisply for greater accuracy. So your complete backswing will be a little shorter.

(3) You should shift your weight back to the left side a little more quickly. This enables you to swing crisply.

(4) The irons follow a more pronounced down-and-through pattern.

(5) Your hands should be a little higher at the finish of the swing. As noted before, the finish position merely shows how well you have observed the proper swing fundamentals. Picture a high finish with the hands, and you'll hit more crisply *through* the ball. At the finish of a good iron swing your hands should be just above the right ear.

Except for the slight differences cited above, the fundamentals outlined in the sections on BACKSWING, DOWNSWING and SWING (GEN-ERAL) relate with equal force to irons and woods. The square stance is advocated for all clubs from the driver down through the 5-iron, so the stance for the 1-iron is square. The smooth and slow start of the downswing that you use for all shots applies also to the 1-iron.

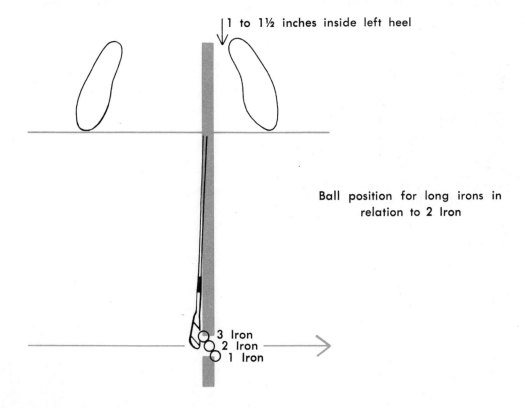

1 to 1½ inches inside left heel

Ball position for long irons in relation to 2 Iron

3 Iron
2 Iron
1 Iron

The formidable reputation of the 1-iron as a difficult club to master explains a number of faults due to anxiety. Tension is reflected for the most part by a hurried, jerky action (instead of a smooth, slow one) at the start of the downswing. Hit smoothly down and through that 1-iron shot. I promise you that the ball will come up nicely and take a reasonably high flight. Don't be intimidated by the club.

1-iron strategy: If you care to take the time and trouble to master the 1-iron, it can become a valuable member of your fourteen-club set. You'll find it particularly valuable on windy days for playing shots into adverse winds. I would recommend that you keep a 1-iron, even though you may not always carry it on a round. On very windy days, use it in place of your 4-wood. Also, practicing with the 1-iron will help you master the 2 and 3-irons. Learn to hit with the 1-iron, and you'll find that the 2 and 3 will seem easier.

One more point about this club: the 1-iron is an excellent trouble-shooter, ideal for shots that must be kept low to avoid hitting over-hanging limbs and the like.

2-iron: This club is the senior member of the standard iron club set. If you can master it, you can control the entire set. Only a few players take to the club naturally, for the 2-iron is the most difficult

The 1 Iron is ideal for shots that must be kept low to avoid hitting overhanging limbs

of the standard irons. (Today the 1-iron is not considered a part of the standard set, which runs from the 2-iron through the 9-iron.)

Part of the difficulty is psychological. The 2-iron has a face loft (20 degrees) comparable to that of the 4-wood. But it doesn't look it. A majority of golfers will say that the 2-iron loft is similar to the 2-wood loft.

A lot of players are afraid that they won't get the ball sufficiently airborne by hitting down-and-through with this club. So they try to give the ball an "assist." The result is faulty hand action—a sort of scooping motion that's fatal to a 2-iron shot. If you're uncertain about the 2-iron, you may also ruin your shot by hitting too fast from the top of the swing.

Part of the difficulty is physical as well. The club is built to hit for distances up to 200 yards for the average-length hitter; it's also designed for accuracy. Therefore the shaft must be fairly long (38½ inches is standard) and the face loft not too great. This means that the clubface hitting area is relatively small and farther away from the eyes and hands (the co-ordinating agents) than is the case with the other irons.

2-iron swing: The 2-iron swing is based on the fundamental principles set forth in the sections on BACKSWING, DOWNSWING and SWING (GENERAL), plus those slight adjustments for the irons used for the 1-iron. These include: (*1*) swinging the club back squarely from the ball in an arc not quite as wide as that used for the woods, (*2*) picking up of the club more abruptly after the takeaway is completed, (*3*) starting the downswing slowly and smoothly, (*4*) shifting the weight more quickly from the right to the left side, (*5*) hitting down-and-through and (*6*) finishing with your hands above your left ear.

The stance for the 2-iron is noticeably narrower than the wood club stance. Because your body rotation is a little more restricted, you don't need quite as wide a base. (It's accuracy you want rather than distance so you shorten the swing.) The backswing is not quite as long nor the finish as full.

Position the ball an inch to an inch and a half nearer the center of the feet from a point even with the left heel. While the ball is still definitely forward of center, it's working back gradually the point where it's in position for the 5-iron. This positioning need not be noticeably different from that used for the 1-iron. The shaft lengths, club-shaft angle (lie) and stroke pattern are virtually the same. Remember that the 1, 2 and 3-irons make the long-iron group. You will find that the swing patterns for the three are almost identical.

Since it requires a great precision to make solid contact with the 2-iron clubface, a perfectly steady head position is absolutely essential. Don't move your head until after the ball is on its way. This is particularly important in long-iron play.

2-iron strategy: You can control the 2-iron if you simply treat it as another iron club. Control your power—never press with the 2-iron. If you don't think you can reach your objective with this club, choose a stronger one and choke down a bit on the grip to reduce the distance. But if you do use the 2-iron while not certain of reaching your goal (for example, in a situation where it's safe to be a little short and dangerous to be slightly off line and hole-high), swing within your maximum power. To attain maximum distance with the 2-iron, you must time your swing to catch the ball solidly in the middle of the clubface. You can't add distance by any additional exertion in the swing.

Be confident. Think in terms of a good shot rather than some real or imagined difficulty. A sound stroke with the 2-iron will produce a good shot; so make up your mind to apply a sound stroke.

3-iron: This is the third member of the long-iron group. Its standard face loft is 23 degrees, the standard length 38 inches. It is half a degree more upright than the 2-iron.

With its slightly shorter shaft length, which calls for a slightly shorter swing, and three more degrees of loft, the 3-iron presents an easier problem than the 2-iron. The extra loft simplifies the problem of lifting the ball. Most golfers can see for themselves that a 3-iron swing down-and-through the ball sends it nicely up and on its way. You don't notice this as readily with the 2-iron.

3-iron swing: The 3-iron stance is square. The ball should be positioned about two inches inside the left heel—a half inch or so nearer the center of the feet than is the case with the 2-iron. Also, the stance position is about a half inch narrower, owing to the slightly shortened swing. Since the 3-iron lie is a little more upright, you stand a shade closer to the ball. This comes naturally because the bottom of the club must be square with the ground and the ball.

3-iron strategy: In all other respects, you use the 3-iron as you would the 2. You can expect ten to fifteen yards less distance than you get with the two. (Note again that I do not specify yardage with these clubs. There are too many variables. Also, the question is not "How far?" but rather "What club do I need?" For 180 yards, one man may require a 2-iron, his partner a 3-iron.)

Your margin for error is likewise an individual matter, though it should decrease as you progress from irons 1 to 9 and the pitching wedge. In other words, you should zero in on the target.

Use the 3-iron if you feel you can reach your goal comfortably. Don't press it.

MIDDLE IRONS

With the middle irons we begin to attack the golf course, so to speak. With the woods, you should plan the next shot, being careful not to take too long a chance. You can allow yourself a fairly wide margin for error with the long irons too. Now and then you should be able to stick a long-iron shot next to the pin and hole the putt—a very satisfying business—but the primary consideration is to position the shot so you can get down in two more.

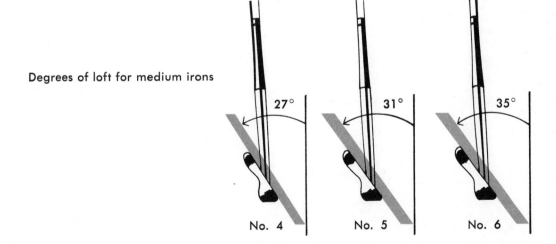

Degrees of loft for medium irons

27°   31°   35°

No. 4   No. 5   No. 6

With the middle irons, you should play away from traps and avoid tough pitches from around the green. But a reasonable mastery of the 4, 5 and 6-irons should enable you to place the ball within twenty or thirty feet of the cup fairly regularly.

The swing with these irons is shorter than the long-iron swing, but the down-and-through pattern is the same.

4-iron: The 4-iron introduces us to the middle-iron range. There is a difference of 4 degrees in the standard face loft of the 4-iron (27 degrees) and the 3-iron (23 degrees). There is a half-inch difference in club length. The standard 4-iron is 37½ inches. The 4-iron is about ¾ of a degree more upright in lie than the 3.

4-iron swing: It follows that the 4-iron swing is a trifle shorter overall than the 3-iron swing, calling for a slightly narrower stance and more limited body rotation. The ball is positioned just forward of the center of the feet, a ball's turn ahead of the centered position for the 5-iron. The stance remains square.

Aside from these minor variations, the swing is no different from the 3-iron swing. And of course, the fundamentals of the swing apply here as elsewhere.

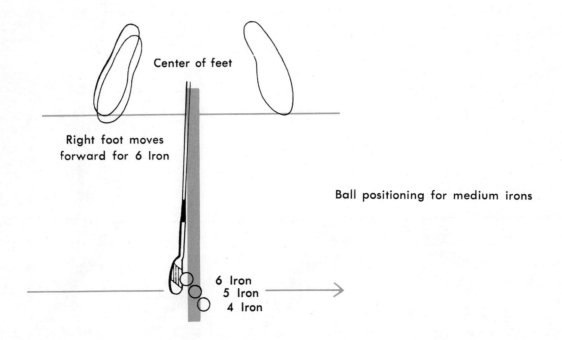

Center of feet

Right foot moves
forward for 6 Iron

Ball positioning for medium irons

6 Iron
5 Iron
4 Iron

The shots are somewhat simpler in the middle-iron range. Loft should no longer be a problem, even an imaginary one. Looking down at the 4-iron from the stance position, you can see plenty of loft built into the face. The swing has become a trifle shorter, and your eyes and hands are closer to the ball. The distance to be covered is ten to fifteen yards less.

4-iron strategy: The middle irons call for a slightly different mental approach than that toward the longer irons. Now the time has come to cut down on the margin left for error. The object of the long irons, remember, is to take the safest possible route to any part of the putting surface. That's the aim on which you base your margin for error. If you would score your best with the middle irons, you should continue to think in terms of "using a lot of green" (*i.e.,* don't flirt with dangerous traps in your quest for the pin and a possible one-putt) but you should try to get the ball in fairly close when the pin is set in a fairly safe part of the green.

Zero in on the target a little more with the middle irons, beginning with the 4-iron.

The strategy outlined here for the 4-iron applies equally to the 5 and 6-irons.

5-iron: This iron is one of the basic golf clubs. Back in the days when only six clubs or so made up a full set, the 5-iron was called a mashie. Midway in the iron set in loft and length, the club is more versatile than most of the other irons.

Therefore, you should practice with this club until you can hit soft, medium and hard 5-iron shots. Once you can gauge these shots, you'll be much more proficient with the middle irons.

5-iron swing: Now that we've reached the midway point for the irons, we ought to check the various swing positions. While discussing the irons, I have referred to these positions as variations of the long-iron positions. Now let's examine the whole picture again.

At address, the ball will be midway between the feet—the position we have gradually been working back to since the driver discussions. The stance for the 5-iron is considerably narrower than the driver position. Your feet are about a foot apart at the instep.

Since the club is shorter and more lofted (5-iron: 31 degrees loft, 36½ inches shaft length), your swing is shorter. Your base need not

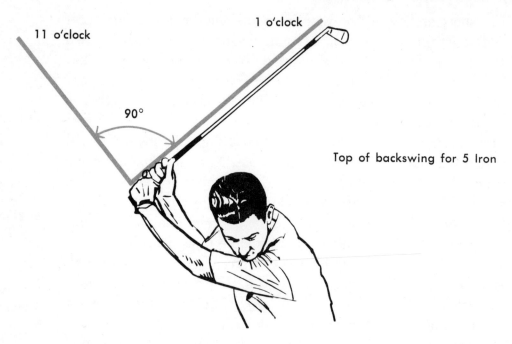

11 o'clock

1 o'clock

90°

Top of backswing for 5 Iron

be as wide, so your stance is narrower. Accuracy is now the prime consideration.

A shorter swing means shorter phases of the swing. The takeaway still moves straight back from the ball and low along the ground, but it's shorter. And the upward movement of the backswing comes a bit sooner and more abruptly.

You can gauge the length of the backswing for the 5-iron by thinking of the club and left arm as forming a right angle at the top. The left arm will point toward 11 o'clock, the club toward one o'clock. With the full driver swing, the clubhead points to three o'clock or directly at the objective.

When you reach the top, start your downswing slowly and smoothly. As it begins, tuck in your right elbow close to the body so that it brushes the right trousers pocket as it goes by.

At the start of the downswing, quickly transfer your weight to your left side to encourage the down-and-through stroke.

This 5-iron swing is strictly for accuracy, though you also need maximum power. Don't jerk or lunge with the mistaken idea of adding distance.

After you meet the ball, the clubhead should continue down-and-through so that it takes out a small divot and then continues straight toward the objective for several inches until the arms are almost fully extended. Finally, you finish with your hands high.

6-iron: The third and most lofted club of the middle-iron group is the 6-iron. It has a face loft of 35 degrees, 4 more than the 5-iron, is a half inch shorter and half a degree more upright in head-shaft angle.

6-iron swing: The stance position begins to open slightly with the 6-iron. The right foot should be about an inch ahead of the left. The open stance tends to restrict body rotation, and since a shorter swing is required for the 6-iron, you don't turn as much as you would for the 5-iron.

The ball position at address is still midway between the feet as in the case of the 5-iron. Actually, you need only open your stance when you pass to the 6-iron. Both clubs are played with virtually the same swing.

With its shorter range, the 6-iron calls for a little more closing in on the target. Cut down a bit on your error margin. The 6-iron range is ten to fifteen yards less than that of the 5-iron.

SHORT IRONS

You'll have to play a great many three-quarter and half shots with the short irons (*see* SCORING RANGE). When the range is 70 to 100 yards, some players may wish to play a full pitching-wedge shot, but it is frequently wiser to play a three-quarter or a half shot with a 7, 8 or 9-iron. The full shot with the pitching wedge goes very high so that it's difficult to control the shot. (To me, the pitching wedge is a special club apart from the regular set.)

You must judge for yourself whether to hit a half shot with a 7-iron or a three-quarter shot with an 8 from, let's say, 85 yards. You'll probably prefer one club over another for purely personal reasons. Whenever the distance is just under the 9-iron range, I like to try to float the ball in with an 8-iron.

You should find practicing with these clubs both pleasant and rewarding. It is quite simple to get a nice, high flight on the ball, which will generally stop quickly after it hits. These shots are pleasant to watch in flight.

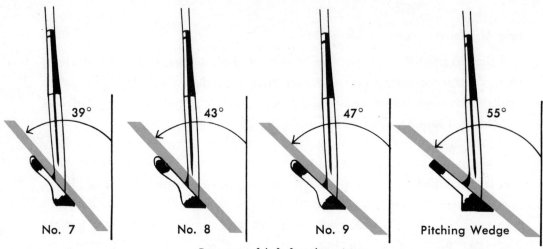

Degrees of loft for short irons

You can save a lot of strokes by mastering the short irons. Practice until you feel you can throw the ball in near the pin with all three of them.

7-iron: When you move into the short-iron range, you should definitely take the offensive. Beginning with the 7-iron, you draw a bead on that pin and think in terms of getting the ball up there for a *possible* one-putt. Even the best short-iron players fail more often than not to set up the one-putt; nevertheless, this should be your objective every time you use a short iron from a fairway lie.

The 7-iron loft is 39 degrees, 4 degrees higher than the 6-iron. The shaft is a half inch shorter, the lie a bit more upright.

7-iron swing: Your stance is slightly more open than it is for the 6-iron, and you should position the ball about a half turn back of center. The open stance restricts body rotation on the short swing and helps you aim the shot. In the open stance you're facing the hole a bit.

Don't use your hands to give the ball added loft. The club has a lot of loft to insure a high flight with plenty of underspin. Just hit down-and-through and keep your head still.

7-iron strategy: In designating the short irons as attack weapons, I don't want to imply that you invariably bang away straight for the pin. If the angle or lie is bad, you will want to play safely for the big part of the green. However, with sufficient practice, you should be able to hit shots no more than ten feet off line. So work toward that end.

8-iron: The 8-iron has 4 degrees more loft than the 7. It is half an inch shorter and a degree more upright. Its range is ten to fifteen yards shorter than the 7-iron range—usually about 120 yards.

Master this club, and you'll cut a lot of strokes off your score. Use the club in a positive manner—you want to get the ball up there for a single putt.

8-iron swing: The swing is virtually a carbon copy of the 7-iron swing. Only a couple of minor adjustments are necessary. Position the ball about a half turn nearer the right foot and open your stance more to conform with the shorter swing.

9-iron: This is the club that was once known as the niblick. Until the advent of the pitching and sand wedges, the 9-iron was the most lofted club in the bag and one of the most frequently used. Nowadays, much of the work formerly done by the 9-iron has been taken over by the two wedges. But the club is still important to the set, and when used properly, it's a great stroke saver.

9-iron swing: Four degrees deeper than the 8-iron, the range of this club is ten to fifteen yards less—normally about 110 yards. A half inch shorter than the 8, the 9 calls for a slightly shorter swing. Hence you position the ball a little more back of center and you open your stance more to restrict body rotation. Otherwise, the 9 swings just like the other two short irons.

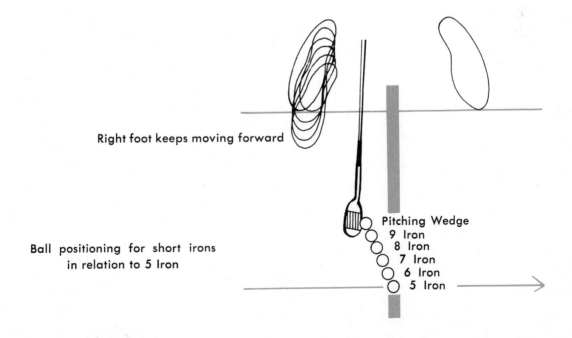

Right foot keeps moving forward

Ball positioning for short irons in relation to 5 Iron

Pitching Wedge
9 Iron
8 Iron
7 Iron
6 Iron
5 Iron

SPECIAL IRONS

Many golfers like to carry a specialized club for run-up shots around the green, etc. Most of these clubs were called jiggers in the old days. Today many of them have special trade names, and their lengths, lofts and lies vary with the manufacturer.

These special clubs are not used so often since the United States Golf Association has limited the number of clubs to fourteen per round. Even the players who have become addicted to them find it's hardly worth leaving out one of the basic clubs in favor of a special model. For example, you can always choke down on the grip of a 4-iron if you want it to approximate the old jigger or run-up iron.

I think that the players who use these specialized clubs use them too often. Faced with a chip-shot problem, they tend to reach for the "old, trusty jigger" without thinking the problem through. (This matter has been taken up under SCORING RANGE.)

SUMMARY

During my travels around the golf tournament circuit and while at home in Memphis, golfers often query me as to the specifications of my own clubs. I think I can best answer their questions and yours

Instead of a Jigger, choke down on the grip of a 4 Iron

right here on paper so that you can relate my experience with equipment to your own individual problems.

I am six feet, two inches tall and weight about 180 when in my best playing condition. My shirt sleeve length is 33 inches, indicating that I have shorter arms than most persons my height, and my hands are somewhat smaller than theirs.

Therefore, I choose clubs with shafts that are three quarters of an inch longer than standard. The overall weight of my clubs is about average, but I prefer a heavier than average swing weight (D-6). I practice and play so often that my hands and golf muscles are stronger than the average player's. Because of my small hands (I can wear golf gloves in either small or medium size, which is unusual for a man of my build), I like grips that are somewhat smaller in circumference.

I feel certain that if my arm length and the size of my hands were in proportion to the rest of my body and if I played about three times a week, I would need standard size clubs with a medium swing weight.

The fourteen clubs I normally carry are a driver, 3-wood, 1 through 9-iron, pitching wedge, sand wedge and putter. I carry a 4-wood to most of my tournaments and occasionally substitute it for my 1-iron. It can come in handy on a course that requires a number of long, high carries when the wind is no problem. I can get about the same distance with my 1-iron and 4-wood if the wind is behaving. Against a strong wind, I pick up a little more distance and a lot more accuracy with my 1-iron. And with a following wind, my 4-wood gives me more distance and nearly equal accuracy.

I generally prefer a 1-iron to a 4-wood because I have the type of golf swing that enables me to get considerable height with my 1-iron. Many players—certainly all players who do not play and practice regularly—find this a difficult feat. Your swing must be grooved more if you want the best results with the 1-iron. The hitting area is considerably smaller than it is on the 4-wood, but with the proper swing, you can achieve accuracy more easily. Since the 4-wood has about twice the loft of a 1-iron (almost equal to a 3-iron), this advantage is more pronounced on shots into a strong wind, when a fairly low trajectory is desirable.

Woods: 1 and 3

Irons: 1—9

Putter

Wedges: Pitching and Sand

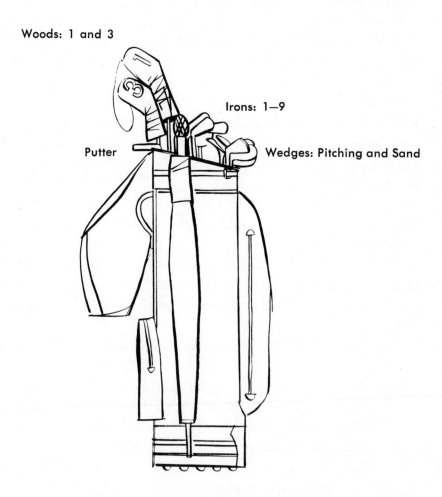

You will note that I carry both a pitching wedge and a sand wedge. I find the sand wedge indispensable because of the heavy flange that makes it "bounce" through the sand. The pitching wedge is invaluable for those grass shots that require a high trajectory and quick stop.

The pitching wedge is especially important for shots from close lies. Actually, the sand wedge would be almost as good for short pitches if we knew that the ball would always be sitting up nicely in the grass. If the lie is a close one, the jutting flange of the sand wedge will keep you from getting under the ball as you must do if you are to keep from blading (half-topping) the shot.

See also PUTTER.

D

DOWNHILL LIES: When your right foot is higher than your left, you must keep from overshifting at the start of the downswing. Otherwise, your body and hands will reach the ball ahead of the clubhead and you'll push the shot. To prevent this fault, put some added weight on your right foot at the start of your swing. Then make an extra effort to shift your weight to the right side on the backswing.

It's hard to loft the ball off a downhill lie. So use a more lofted club than you would from a level lie. The next higher number should be used for average downhill lies. But if the grade is exceptionally steep, choose a club two or more numbers higher.

When the ground is higher behind the ball than below it, you'll reach the bottom of your swing early. Compensate by positioning the ball about an inch nearer your right foot.

DOWNSWING: First, let's look at the downswing as a unit. You want a smooth, unhurried start, then a gradual acceleration of club-

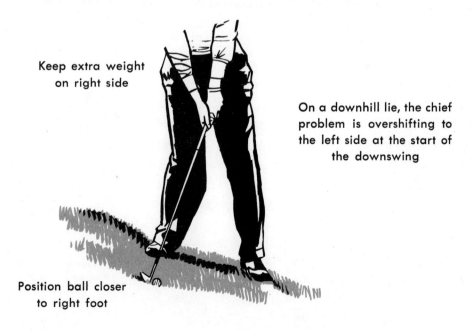

Keep extra weight
on right side

On a downhill lie, the chief
problem is overshifting to
the left side at the start of
the downswing

Position ball closer
to right foot

head speed that reaches its peak upon contact. The clubhead approaches the ball on a straight line low along the ground and passes through it for several inches before sweeping to a balanced finish. And during the entire swing your head remains in the address position.

You complete the downswing in a fraction of a second with no time for corrections. You must rivet your full attention on hitting the ball solidly. Therefore, it's important to *start* the downswing properly.

A number of actions take place simultaneously as the swing begins —the hips start to turn back to the left, you shift your weight back to the left foot, your left arm sets up a slight downward pull and your right elbow is tucked in close to the body so that it will almost brush the right hand trousers pocket as it passes. These actions cannot be separated in actual performance, but you can isolate them in your mind for a fuller appreciation of how each part operates.

FIRST DOWNSWING MOVEMENT

A number of theories have been advanced as to what the first movement of the downswing should be. Some say a downward pull or tug with the left arm. Others go for the backward turn of the left hip to the left. Still another theory maintains that Step A consists of a quick weight transfer to the left foot.

Each of these theories is logical, but they are still gimmicks or artificial aids. They do not allow the golfer to think of the swing as a single, natural action.

The fact is that each of these recommended "first movements" has its own consequences. Try it yourself. Give a little downward tug with your left arm and note that this action pulls the left hip back to the left and tips your weight back over the left foot. Each of these actions encourages the others. And all of these actions are accomplished simultaneously.

THE SLOW START

You should think of the beginning of the downswing as a unified action that includes the arm tug, hip turn and weight transfer. But the single unified action is an uncoiling or swiveling of the body.

Starting the downswing too fast is the great swing-wrecker of golf. And unfortunately, the only advice I can offer is "Don't do it!"

Over-anxiousness and a desire to see the ball nicely on its way are mainly responsible for a hasty downswing. And like the hasty backswing, it happens most easily and frequently in the tough situations —when it hurts the most.

As a matter of fact, the too eager downswing is harder to overcome than the rapid backswing because the problem crops up in the middle of the action. The golfer can often solve his backswing problem by convincing himself that he shouldn't swing back too fast. But he becomes over-anxious at the top of his swing despite himself and tries to apply his power from the top down.

The best way to overcome this tendency is to think the swing through at the start. Imagine a smooth, unhurried beginning to your

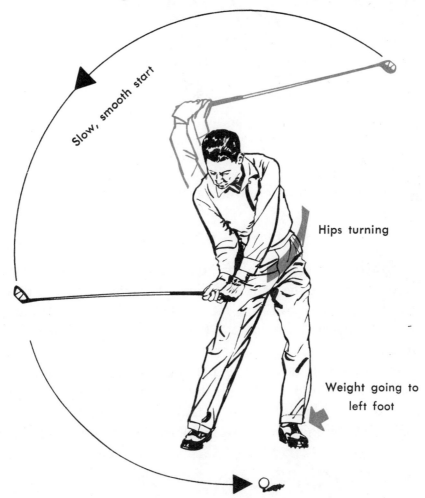

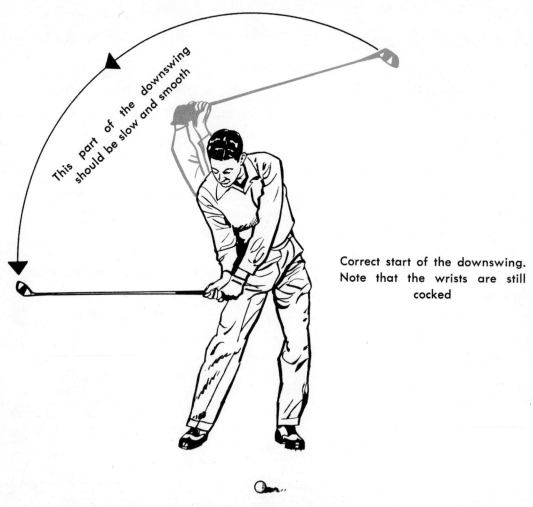

This part of the downswing should be slow and smooth

Correct start of the downswing. Note that the wrists are still cocked

downswing. Recognize the strong tendency to start down too fast, and then concentrate on overcoming it.

RIGHT ELBOW AND HIP

If there is a "secret" to the golf swing, it lies in keeping the right elbow in close to the body and inside the right hip on the downswing. In no other way can you hit the ball with an inside-out pattern, which is the way you *must* hit if it you are to achieve power and accuracy.

In the correct downswing pattern, the clubhead approaches the ball from the inside: *i.e.*, with the clubhead about two feet from the ball, it is traveling at an angle that would send the ball out to the right. But you square the angle with the ball in order to hit it straight.

Right elbow in close, brushing by the right pocket

Right elbow inside right hip

Inside-out swing

The opposite or incorrect approach to the ball is outside-in: *i.e.,* across the ball from right to left. This incorrect pattern is brought about when the right hip gets in the way of the right elbow, forcing it up and out, which in turn shifts the plane of the swing and makes the outside-in route the only one open to the clubhead.

Keep that right elbow tucked in close and inside the right hip. We saw in the section on the BACKSWING that the right hip must turn out if the right elbow is to stay inside. The two actions are combined.

When I am hitting the ball at my best, I can always feel that my right elbow has brushed right by my right side trousers pocket.

HITTING AREA

When the hands pass below the belt line on the downswing, you are entering what is known as the hitting area. This is the time to apply full power, but don't lunge or jump at the ball. Just concentrate on hitting straight through it. Remember that in the proper golf swing the clubhead speed builds gradually. So don't try to hurry the hit.

Right hip forcing
right elbow out
and away from
body

Incorrect outside-in swing

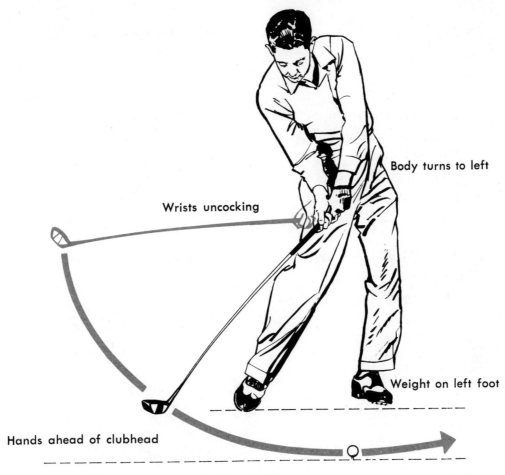

Body turns to left

Wrists uncocking

Weight on left foot

Hands ahead of clubhead

The Hitting Area

The power needed at this stage of the swing comes from uncoiling your hips and shoulders left and back, shifting your weight back to the left foot and uncocking the wrists. This power or clubhead speed is derived from what engineers call a torque action and increases only so long as the clubhead remains behind the hands on the downswing.

Be sure to keep your hands ahead of the clubhead until the last possible moment when it must catch up and meet the ball. Any sudden attempt to supply extra power with the hands through the hitting area not only fails to add speed to the clubhead but is likely to detract from your power by moving the clubhead from its proper path—square to the ball.

When you try to kill the ball, you have everything to lose and nothing to gain. So stay steady-on and meet the ball solidly with the clubhead.

POSITION AT CONTACT

Your position at contact can be analyzed as follows:

(1) Head in the same position as it was at the start of the swing —and anchored.

(2) Right elbow tucked in close to the body and inside the right hip.

(3) Hands in the same position as at the start of the swing.

(4) Left arm straight and firm, forming a generally straight line with the shaft from the left shoulder to the ball.

(5) Weight over on your left side with your left foot planted solidly on the ground.

(6) Right side relaxed.

(7) Left hip turned well around and out of the way of the hands and continuing to turn.

Position at contact

Muscular tension in right side
causes falling back

(8) Shoulders turned back parallel to the line of flight with the right shoulder about four inches under the left.

(9) Eyes riveted on the back of the ball.

A close study of this breakdown is rewarding, but you must remember that the position is fluid, not static.

Although nearly all your weight is on the left side, it is still behind the ball at impact. You are simply uncoiling your body without swaying forward.

RELAXED RIGHT SIDE

Your right side is relaxed as you hit the ball. In fact, it can be said that the right side collapses. If there's any muscular tension on that side as you come into the ball, you'll lose power. At this point, the right side should be flowing into and through the ball, adding its weight to your total power.

Any muscular tension on that side makes you fall back from the ball, and you lose a lot of power and accuracy.

The last positive action of the right side occurs just as you reach the hitting area. You push slightly off the right toe, while your right knee and hip exert some force to keep the left hip turning to the left. After that, the right side simply relaxes and goes along for the ride.

CLUBHEAD PAST THE BALL

The clubhead should continue in a straight line parallel to the intended line of flight for several inches past the ball.

Ball and clubhead remain in contact for about two inches following impact. (Long enough for the ball to flatten out a bit against the clubface and then bounce off the face, as it were.) The duration of this contact affects the direction and height of the shot.

If the clubface is turned in or out, the ball will take off with a left or right spin, and you'll get a hook or a slice. Also, the ball will go up the face of the club in varying degrees, depending on the angle of loft of the clubface.

Hence the importance of keeping the clubface square to the line of flight and low along the ground for several inches following impact.

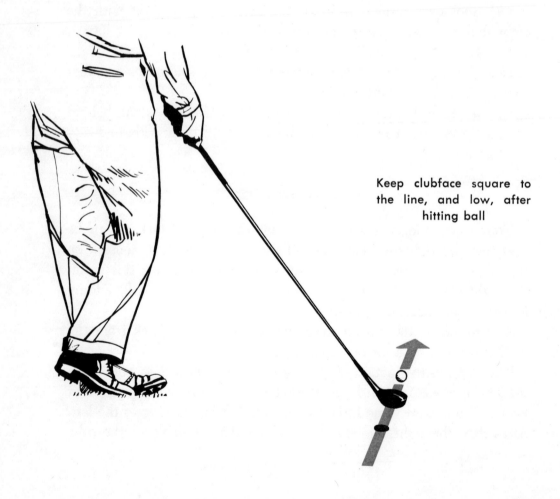

Keep clubface square to the line, and low, after hitting ball

Head being pulled around
by the force of the swing

The longer you can keep the clubhead square, the smaller is your margin of error in the swing. If the clubhead starts upward too abruptly after contact, the ball is likely to go too high. This cuts down on distance and adds to the problem of control.

But if you can keep it low along the ground, it will be easier to hold the clubhead square to the line of flight.

HEAD PULLED AROUND—NOT LIFTED

In a good, effective golf swing, your head remains firmly stationary until after the ball is met. Then when the club shaft is parallel to the ground and your hands begin to roll over, the natural force of the swing will pull your head around to a position from which you can follow the ball's flight.

"Keep your head down" has always been a sage admonition. The Scotsmen used to say, "Look for a sixpence where the ball was." It has often been advocated that the player should count three after the ball is hit before looking up from the impact spot.

Such freely offered golf tips are based on sound logic but tend to overemphasize their point. Or to put it another way, the medicine is good, but taken in too strong a dosage it can be more harmful than helpful.

I can safely say that if it were effective to keep the head down for several seconds after the ball is hit, you would see a great many playing professionals with eyes glued to the ground until long after the shot has been made. But you don't. They know that a good swing pulls the head around, and they let it do just that. They do try to avoid moving the head prematurely—before the swing pulls it around—but that is another matter entirely.

I feel that most players will find it helpful to slightly exaggerate keeping down of the head until after the ball is well on its way. This slight exaggeration will counteract the natural tendency to look up too quickly. But don't overdo it.

Golf is a game of *doing* without *overdoing*.

ARM EXTENSION ON FOLLOW-THROUGH

You should be able to tell whether you have made a good swing at that point in the follow-through when your arms are fully extended

Club parallel to ground

Proper height for teeing up ball for drive

and the club is parallel to the ground, pointing straight toward your objective. It is, of course, a fluid position. You should not think of arresting any motion at this point. But at the beginning of the swing you will find it helpful to think of this follow-through position.

At this position your hands should begin to roll over and your head turn so that you can follow the ball. If you reach this position naturally in the swing, it will mean that you have hit through the ball and swung past a stationary head. To play golf effectively, you should do both these things.

DRIVER: The driver or 1-wood is one of the two most important clubs you have in your bag; the other is your putter. On most golf courses you will use the driver thirteen to fifteen times per round. You will probably use it from the tee on all the par-4 and par-5 holes and occasionally on a long par-3.

Thus you can see that you'll be using the driver only slightly less than the putter. That fact in itself tells a great deal about the importance of your driver in scoring your best. However, the frequency with which you use the driver is only a part of the story.

These are the important points to remember about the driver: (1) Select it carefully because of its prime importance to your game and its frequent use. (2) Use it with intelligence and finesse rather than as an instrument for attaining distance only. And (3) leave it in the bag occasionally even when maximum distance is desirable, because accuracy and safety is even more necessary.

The driver should always be included among the fourteen clubs the United States Golf Association rules permit you to carry. The club is simply too important to be left out. You can never hope to play your best golf unless you learn to use the driver. The driver is not so difficult a club that you should give up on it, as might be the case with a 1 or even a 2-iron.

One thing more in connection with the driver: tee the ball high enough to get the whole clubface on the ball with a sweeping stroke. Teeing the ball too low will induce a downward type of stroke that will not give you the best results with this club.

SELECTION

Because of its great importance to your overall game, your driver should be selected with the utmost care. It is the key club in choosing your set of woods.

If you are driving as well as you think you should, keep the driver you have and leave it as it is. But if you are driving badly, you should probably change drivers or get your professional to alter the one you have. In this connection, here are some driver facts to guide you:

The standard driver length for men is 41½ to 43 inches. The normal weight range is from 12½ to 14 ounces. Generally speaking, there are three types of shafts—flexible (whippy), medium and stiff. The normal driver loft is 10 degrees.

We have seen earlier in the chapter that unless your build varies greatly from the norm, one of the standard lengths should accommodate you.

Regardless of your build, one of the standard weights should be suited to you and your swing. Among the playing professionals, whose company includes the big, the little and the medium sized, there are virtually no departures from these standard driver weights. You should remember that if your driver is a little too heavy for you to swing effectively, you will be sacrificing a great deal of clubhead speed, which is the basis of power (distance).

If your swing is slow and deliberate, you will probably want a driver with the most flexible of the three types of shafts. If your swing is of medium speed, your logical choice will be a shaft of medium flexibility. If your swing is short and fast, get a driver with the stiff type of shaft. You should be stronger than most if the stiff-shaft driver is to be the one for you.

If you tend to have trouble getting the ball up, you may find it expedient to have your professional add a degree or two of loft to the face of your driver. There are, on the average, three degrees of loft difference between your driver and your 2-wood. You might better solve the loft problem by adding a little more slant to the driver instead of substituting the 2-wood for the driver off the tee.

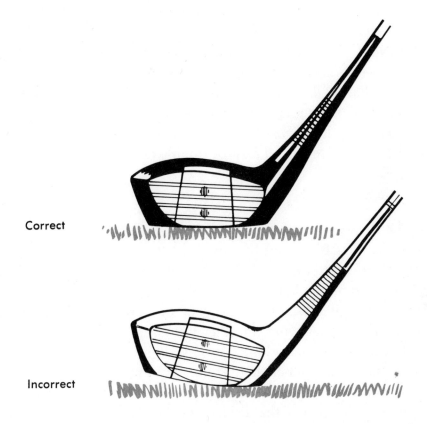

Correct

Incorrect

Similarly, if you think you need to keep your drives down a bit more, have the professional take out a bit of the loft. Not many golfers, however, are beset by this problem.

Actually, you can best select your driver by "feel." If the club *feels* like one with which you can best drive, the chances are it is. If the one you have is deficient in this proper feel, the chances are it is for one of the reasons outlined above.

To repeat, the selection of your driver is a highly important matter in reducing your golf score to a happy minimum and increasing your enjoyment of the game.

There is one other factor to be considered in your selection of the right driver. That is the lie—or the angle formed by the shaft and the head. The only point you need consider here is whether the clubhead rests squarely on the ground when placed there for the start of your normal swing. It should rest no more on the toe of the club than on the heel. But this is easily determined by the look and the feel.

DRIVING: When you are standing on the tee with your driver, you are about to make the opening move in your battle with the hole ahead. The way in which you make that opening move will determine the kind of flight that lies ahead—either an offensive or defensive, a winning or losing battle. A bad drive can cost you a number of strokes and cause you all sorts of trouble on the hole ahead.

SWING

The driver swing is the basic swing. Specific points to be remembered particularly about the driver swing are that the full shot with the driver calls for the fullest body turn (pivot), the greatest transfer of weight from the left side to the right on the backswing, the longest swing arc and the highest lifting of the left heel off the ground to complete the backswing. In other words, it's your biggest swing.

Ball positioning at address is only slightly more important on the drive than on any other shot. The reason that ball positioning is more important with the driver is that you get greater distance with that club. And the greater the distance of your shot, the more your errors in ball positioning will show up.

I position the ball for the drive just even with the instep of the left foot, as do most other playing professionals. The idea is to have the ball placed as exactly as possible at the end of the downswing—or just at the end of the level sweep of the clubhead—before it starts upward in the follow-through. You see, the driver swing is a sweep. All the other swings (except the putting stroke) are at least slightly downward in direction.

You may find it helpful to alter this positioning just a little bit. If you tend to slice, you may find it helpful to move the ball forward to a point, say, just inside the left toe. Conversely, if you tend to hook, you might experiment by moving the ball back a little nearer the center point between the feet. But the alteration should be very slight. If you change the position to any considerable degree, you will have less chance to execute a good golf swing.

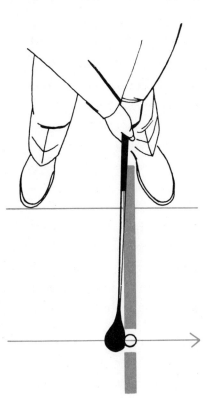

Ball position for driver   Driver swing is a "sweep"

Once you have established just the best ball positioning for your drive, be very careful to use it consistently. It is a highly important part of your driving. Carelessness in this department can result in general wildness off the tee, and it will certainly cause an inconsistent pattern in your driving.

Except for this ball positioning and the fact that the driver swing is a complete sweep, the stroke with the driver is in basic conformity with the swing for the rest of the clubs (*see* BACKSWING, DOWNSWING *and* FINISH OF THE SWING).

STRATEGY

Sound planning on tee shots is one of the most important steps toward lower golf scores. It is also, I have noted, one of the most neglected.

Far too many golfers regard tee-shot placement too lightly. They are keen enough—often too keen—about distance. But they tend toward carelessness or indifference when it comes to the important phase of the tee-shot that calls for the kind of advance planning that will simplify the second shot.

There are two conditions on which a "good" tee-shot depends: good distance and good placement. You need the distance in order to be near enough to the hole to reach it with the subsequent shot; you need the good placement in order to have a clear and simple route by which you can reach the hole.

Good placement involves two considerations: safety and getting the ball in proper position for the next play. Unless you are an extremely accurate driver, you must leave yourself a margin for error in your tee shots. Do not skirt too close to out-of-bounds lines, even if it means getting into position for the simplest second shot possible. You must keep the ball in play. You should get that drive in the right position from which to play the next shot. Always think ahead.

It has often occurred to me that too many golfers (including myself at times) refuse to think on the golf course until forced to do so by the circumstances. Put them in deep rough or behind a tree, and they really bear down and start thinking about how to get out of a tough situation. But too few of us seem to realize—until too late at least— that intelligent planning would probably have kept us out of trouble in the first place.

Don't forget that driving is more than an effort to gain the greatest possible distance in the general direction of the hole. You must also think ahead to the next shot and the play of the entire hole.

Below are some sample driving problems that emphasize this attitude:

Situation: The hole is 460 yards, measured along the middle of the fairway, and is par-five. If you care to risk hugging the left side of the fairway, you can cut off up to about thirty yards of distance. But a small creek runs along the left side of the fairway, and across the creek is the woods. The fairway is wide with plenty of room to the right. But the right hand route adds to the yardage. The creek along the left side turns and cuts in front of the green so that the second shot will be quite risky even with a good long drive, should you decide to try to reach the green in two.

Solution: Let's consider the problem first from the standpoint of the low-handicap golfer who is a good driver. His best bet is to aim for the middle of the fairway, leaving open the decision as to whether to try to get on in two or play safe short of the creek. If he happens

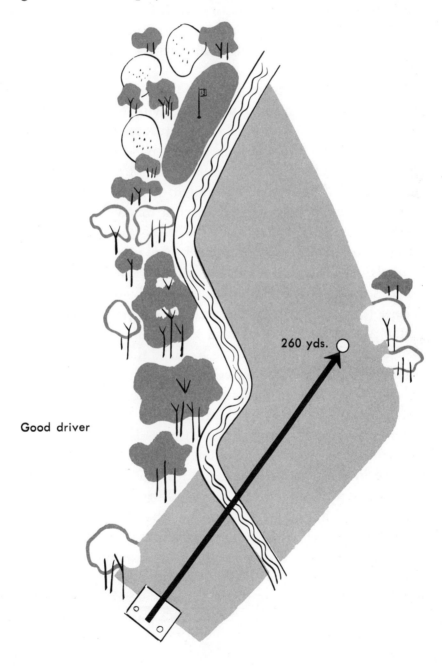

260 yds.

Good driver

to turn his drive a little left and get good distance, he can then elect
to try for the green. Otherwise not. If you are this golfer, you will find
that some days your driving will be good so that you feel you can place
your drives just about as you want them. However, you should not let
this feeling lull you into overconfidence so that you take unwarranted
chances. You should always leave a margin for error of about twenty
yards when you're using the driver. This is about the degree of accuracy that even the best drivers can normally expect. To repeat: a
normally good driver should play this drive for the middle of the
fairway.

Now the problem as it applies to the average or medium-handicap
golfer: If you are a golfer of average driving talent, you should always
favor the right side of the fairway on this tee shot. You should say to
yourself on the tee that you mean to depend on a good third shot so
that you can have a putt for your birdie four. A drive of exceptional
length and fortunate placement *might possibly* put you in a position
where you can try to get on in two. But this will seldom happen. And
the average player should take such breaks as they come and not take
unwarranted chances in trying to set them up.

In planning the play of the hole before hitting the drive, the average
player should keep in mind that there will be one chance that he *must*
take: lofting the ball over the creek to reach the green. It's almost a
certainty that he'll have to take this inevitable chance on the third
shot, so he should plan the hole to make that third shot as short and
simple as possible. This strategy calls for safety tactics on the drive.
When you know you must take *one* chance on a hole, do not gra-
tuitously throw in *another* risky situation.

Now let's consider the high-handicap golfer. He must always favor
the right side in a driving situation of this type. Furthermore, he may
be wise in using his 2-wood instead of his driver to get the ball up
and hit a part of the fairway. He should reason that two of his better
shots will put him in position to clear the creek on his third and get
on in three, which is the number of strokes that will be required by
all but a very few of the better golfers in reaching this green.

Our high-handicapper should note that here is a hole that gives him
one of his best chances to play on nearly equal terms with his golfing
betters. Note the difference if the creek were not where it is fronting

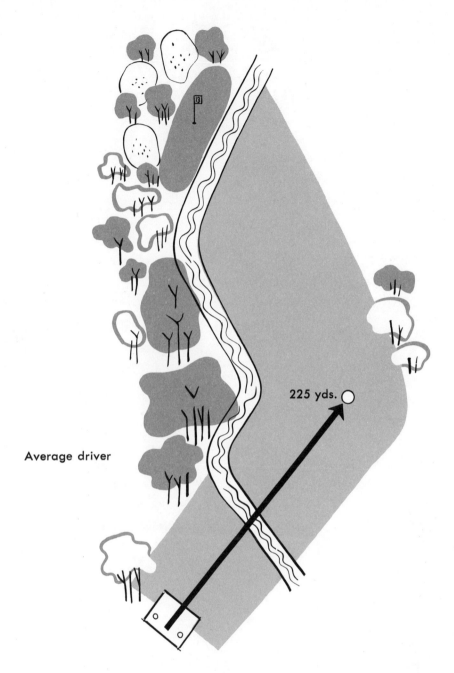

225 yds.

Average driver

the green. The better players could go all out to get on in two, a feat which would be beyond the capabilities of the high-handicapper even if the creek were not there. The creek becomes the equalizer. So to compete successfully against players of lower handicap, the high-handicap golfer must recognize and take advantage of the holes whose design and length make them more suited than most to his style of play.

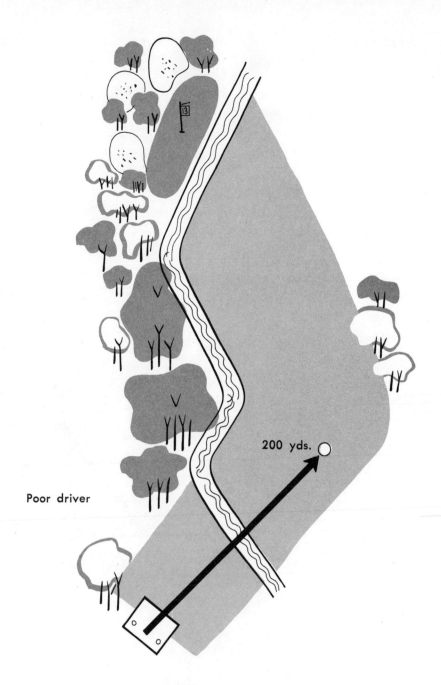

Poor driver

200 yds.

The high-handicap player should be cautious on the tee-shot on this hole. He should be most careful not to destroy the chance he has of getting on the green in three.

The hole described in the preceding driving exercises is the justly famous No. 13 at the Augusta National Golf Course, one of the best holes on this great course. Note that it permits you to bite off as much as you think you can chew and that it lets you choose the size of the stakes if you care to gamble. Assuming, for example, you want to cut off distance by hugging the left side of the fairway on the drive, you can set up a fairly easy second shot at the risk of a one-stroke penalty for cutting it too close and winding up in the ditch. If you play the drive fairly and then decide to try carrying the creek and reaching the green as your second shot, the risk will be greater. In short, the hole sets up a very fair system of rewards and penalties. That is the ideal of golf course architecture—the reward for a successful shot should be commensurate with the risk you are required to take. The penalty for an unsuccessful shot is severe but fair.

The Augusta No. 13 offers virtually limitless possibilities for the study of intelligent driving practices. In addition, it calls for sound thinking all the way until you sink the final putt on the hole.

Situation: The hole is 370 yards, par-four. The fairway is relatively narrow, about 40 yards across, as befits a relatively short two-shot hole. Out-of-bounds is on the right, beginning about ten yards from the right edge of the fairway. On the left is rough plus a few trees and a deep bunker near the left edge of the fairway about 240 yards from the tee. The right side of the fairway offers the best second-shot angle for hitting the middle of the green. A shot from the left rough must carry a sand trap at the left front corner of the green. There are more traps on the right side, and the green is elevated on both sides and at the back.

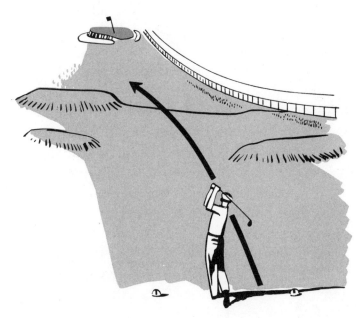

Solution: Even the best drivers should slightly favor the left side of the fairway here since out-of-bounds is to be shunned always. However, they should not do so through fear. Golf is not a game to be played with a craven attitude. It is plain good sense to play slightly away from out-of-bounds at all times, and playing for the left half of the fairway on this type of hole offers the best chance of getting a par, which is the score to keep in mind.

Note that if you play the drive too far to the left, the trees, the bunker and the rough lie in wait to exact a proper penalty. Moreover, you will be left with a second shot across a sand trap, and your angle will be a tough one.

The preceding situation points up the lesson that the way you are driving on the particular day in question should be taken into account in planning your driving strategy. The hole in question is the seventh at the Colonial Country Club in Memphis. By the time you reach the seventh hole, you should have a good idea about how you are handling your driver on that round. All players have on-days and off-days with the driver just as they do with the putter and the other clubs. If you have noticed a tendency to push or slice the ball as you work your way along to No. 7, you should be more than ordinarily cautious about that out-of-bounds threat. And if you have been hooking or pulling, take that into account.

The lesson here is that you must *think* before hitting the drive. This hole offers a particularly striking example of this fact.

Situation: A short par-four, 310 yards, with a very narrow fairway that becomes narrower as the green is approached. Trees and heavy rough line each side of the fairway. Traps guard the small island green.

Solution: This hole reminds us that at times the best "use" of the driver is to leave it in the bag and substitute a 3-wood or long iron. Note that the danger increases with the distance the shot travels from the tee, since the fairway becomes quite narrow near the green.

Take all factors into consideration. If your normal driving pattern is short but accurate, take your driver and hit away, being careful to line up the shot well before you swing. But if you are long off the tee and tending to wildness, eschew the driver in favor of, say, a 2-iron. The chief idea is that two shots will be required to reach the green

A hooked 2 Iron stays in the fairway while a long wood ends up in the trees

under the best of circumstances. So be certain that you have a second shot that offers at least a fair opportunity of getting the ball on the green. Do not risk all on a tee-shot in an inherently dangerous situation.

E

EQUIPMENT: *See* CLUBS

EXPLOSION SHOT: The non-sand explosion shot is played from grass or bare ground. You use the same technique you'd use to explode the ball out of the sand: *i.e.*, you hit an inch or two behind the ball with a fairly hard swing and "explode" it up and onto the green.

Don't try this shot until all other possibilities have been ruled out. It is a hard shot to bring off, though not as hard as you might think at first.

The Non-Sand Explosion Shot
from a buried lie in deep
grass

A very close or partially buried lie may challenge you to try this shot. The lie would offer you little or no chance of getting under the ball and lofting it with a normal pitch shot.

Have you ever tried to hit a full pitching-wedge shot and accidentally hit an inch or so behind the ball? And didn't the ball rise up lazily and travel only a few yards in the air? Well, this is the same kind of shot I am prescribing here. Only you do deliberately what you have done accidentally.

The best club for this shot is the pitching wedge. You need its sharp leading edge to dig into the ground and get under the ball. The sand wedge with its flanged bottom may bounce forward on striking the ground and send the ball scudding over the green or into the bank. As with the sand explosion, you make no actual contact between ball and clubface. That is the prime condition of an explosion shot.

Pick the spot where you want the clubhead to enter the ground, and keep your eye on that spot. Before you swing, decide how much power you think you'll need. Then try to apply just that amount of power to the swing.

For the sand explosion shot see SAND TRAPS.

EYE DISCIPLINE: *See* LOOKING UP

F

FINISH OF THE SWING: Obviously, the completion of your golf swing has nothing directly to do with the spot where the ball comes to rest. The ball is well on its way, for better or for worse, long before the completion of your follow-through.

However, the finish *does* indicate how well you have carried out the swing fundamentals that *do* determine the ball's flight and stop-

Finish of the full swing

ping place. Thus a knowledge of the right finish adds to your understanding of the swing itself.

At the completion of a full swing, your weight is over on the left side, your right side is relaxed, your hips are turned so that your body faces the objective, your head is turned so that your eyes are in a position to follow the flight of the ball, your hands are above and slightly behind the left ear and you are well balanced.

You will find it helpful to think ahead to the completion of your swing. Imagine your hands finishing high while your body is facing the objective and you are still perfectly balanced. If you give some thought to these aims *before* you start the swing, you'll improve your complete swing.

A pretty finish has nothing to do with it. Avoid being what is sometimes called a "studio player" who strives to look good on the swing. You want to *be* good while finishing gracefully and effectively (*see* DOWNSWING, PUTTING *and* SAND TRAPS).

FOLLOW-THROUGH: *See* DOWNSWING, PUTTING *and* SAND TRAPS

FORWARD PRESS: *See* BACKSWING

G

GRIP: Any complete discussion of the golf swing must logically start with the grip. Obviously the grip is the only contact between the swinger and the club. A proper grip, which permits correct hand action, can compensate for some faulty movement of the body during the swing, but proper body movements cannot compensate for the faulty hand action caused by an improper grip. Thus a proper grip is absolutely basic to a good golf swing.

The grip might be compared to the hinges on a door. If the hinges are properly placed and in good working order, the door will open

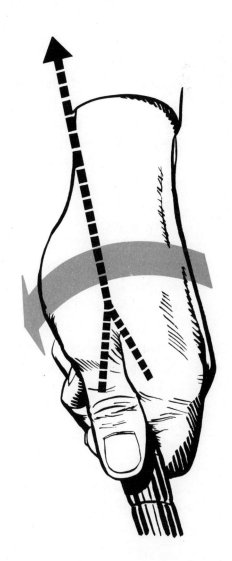

and shut smoothly and properly. The same is true of the swing. The hands must be so placed on the club that they will permit the club-head to move back along the right path and return to the ball squarely. They must be firm enough on the club to retain control, yet loose and supple enough to allow for a free swing without jerkiness.

If it were only necessary to pull back the club a few inches, almost any sort of a grip would do. Hence the number of variations in putting grips with one working about as well as another. But on the full swing, which must combine power and accuracy, you must adhere to the proper fundamentals of gripping.

A proper grip involves two factors: (1) Proper placing of the hands on the club. (2) Application of the proper pressure.

PLACING LEFT HAND ON THE CLUB

Keep in mind that the left hand grip involves the fingers and the palm. With the left arm extended as it would be at the position of address, lay the handle of the club diagonally across the fingers and palm of the left hand. The handle should lay across the middle joint of the index finger and should meet the palm of the hand at the base of the middle finger. It should extend diagonally so that it lies just under the callus pad in the heel of the hand.

Then just fold your hand around the grip of the club and simply grip it. Now we can check to see if you have placed your left hand properly. If you have, you should be able to look straight down and see two knuckles, one belonging to the index finger and the other the middle finger. The back of this hand will be pointing in the general direction of your objective.

The left thumb should be down the shaft, just to the right of center of the top of the shaft. The thumb and the index finger will then form a V. This V should be pointing just to the right of the chin—almost straight up but just slightly to the right of vertical.

PLACING RIGHT HAND ON THE CLUB

Now bring your right hand to the club and place it so that the handle of the club lies along the third joint of the index, middle and

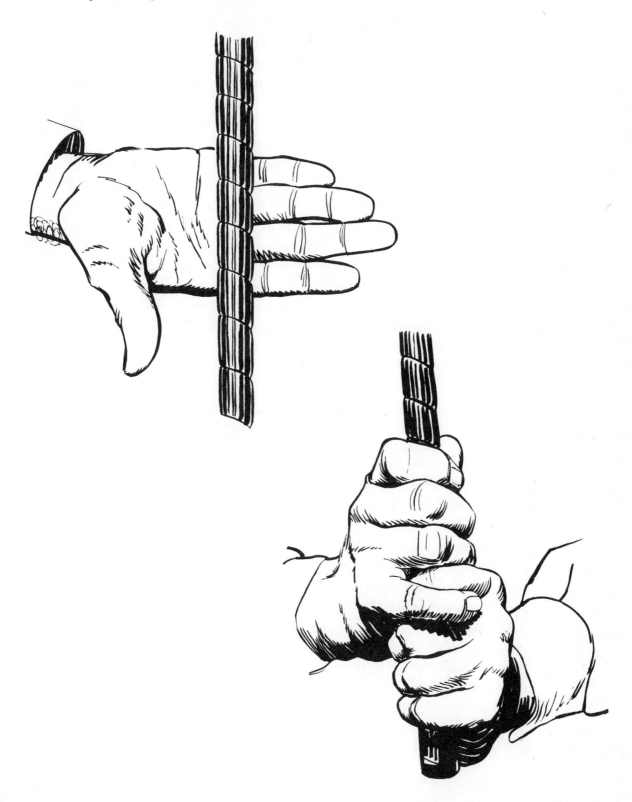

ring fingers. The little finger of the right hand wraps around the index finger of the left. It may wrap around the top of this index finger or lay in the groove between the index and middle fingers of the left hand. That is a matter of individual preference, of what feels right to you. The idea is to get the little finger of the right hand out of the way so as to equalize the power of the two hands on the club and unify the two hands so they can work better together.

Fold the right hand over so that the left thumb fits in the groove at the base of the right hand. The right thumb will be down the shaft and just over to the left of center of the top of the shaft. The tip of the right thumb will extend just beyond the tip of the right index finger, almost meeting it.

In this position, the thumb and index finger of the right hand will form a V, just as the thumb and index finger of the left hand do. The two V's will form a continuous line pointing barely to the right of the chin. Looking down, you will be able to see the first knuckle of the right hand and only that knuckle.

Study the illustrations, and make your grip conform.

VARIATIONS FOR STRAIGHT SHOTS

There are two variations of this standard grip that have been used with success. One is identical with the standard grip here described except that the little finger of the right hand and the index finger of the left hand interlock rather than overlap. In the other, the left thumb is around the shaft instead of resting on it.

I see no reason to use the former of these two variations unless you just happen to feel more comfortable with the little finger of the right hand interlocked with the index finger of the left. Let your individual preference decide. It does not actually alter the basic grip.

Placing the left thumb around the shaft might be helpful to players with very small hands. But I would suggest that instead of using this grip, such players have the grips of their clubs made smaller in circumference so they can use the standard grip with the thumb down the shaft.

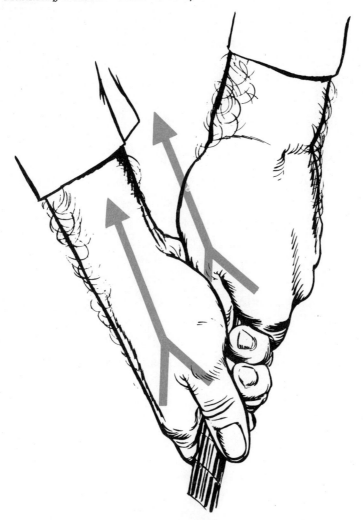

VARIATIONS FOR DELIBERATE HOOKS AND SLICES

To facilitate hitting a deliberate slice when that type of flight is desired, move both hands to the left so that when you look down, you see only one knuckle of the left hand and two knuckles of the right hand.

For the deliberate hook, reverse the turn of the hands so you can see three knuckles on the left hand and none on the right.

These grip variations are more fully described under HOOK SHOT and SLICE.

PRESSURE

Some golf experts have expressed the thought that grip is the wrong word to apply to the method of holding the club. They think the term suggests the application of too much pressure with the hands—a hard hold on the club.

I think the club should be held as firmly as possible without setting up any undue tension in the muscles of the forearms. Firmness of grip depends on the right "touch" or "feel."

A firm grip is necessary at the moment the clubhead meets the ball. Otherwise the clubhead will be turned by the force of the impact, and you'll lose both power and direction. But this does not necessarily mean the club must be held as firmly at the start as it is at impact. You will unconsciously grip the club firmly as you come into the ball; your muscles will naturally tighten up before impact.

Contrariwise, if you try to grip the club too firmly at the outset of the swing, chances are you will relax somewhat before contact and meet the ball too loosely.

The "Piccolo Grip" at the
top of the backswing

Grip the club firmly but gently, as you would a baseball for a long throw. Maintain a steady, even pressure until you reach the hitting area on the downswing. Then depend on your muscles to add the pressure you will need on contact.

One of the major grip faults is loosening the hands at the top of the swing (the "piccolo grip"). Don't do this if you want accuracy. Hold onto the club with an even pressure in both hands. If you let go at all, you'll be lucky to get the club back to its address position when you tighten the grip in anticipation.

Many players find it hard to grip the club with the last three fingers of the left hand at the top of the swing. Therefore, they wonder if they should grip it tighter at address with these fingers than the rest. I don't believe they should. If you try to grip harder with these three fingers at the start, you will be more inclined to relax them a bit at the top of the swing. Hold the club firmly at the top, but don't exert extra pressure at the start.

If you find yourself forced to relax your grip a bit at the club top in order to complete the backswing, chances are your backswing is too long. Shorten it enough so you'll have a firm grip at the top.

Of course, your short chip grip will not be as firm as the one used for a full drive. The difference is slight, but it can be sensed.

H

HALF SHOTS: *See* SCORING RANGE

HEADWINDS: *See* WIND

HEELING: The heeled shot is obviously related to the shank. You hit the ball with the club heel—not on the shaft but too near it. The usual result is a considerable loss of power. The ball will head left, but the small amount of slice will bring it back fairly close to the intended line of flight. Power is lost because only a fraction of the clubhead weight is behind the ball at impact.

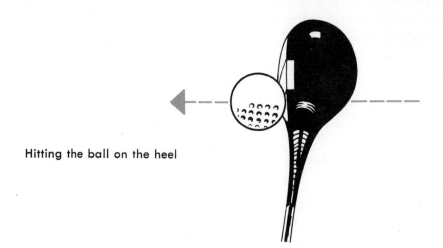

Hitting the ball on the heel

Since heeling and shanking result from the same causes, the cure is essentially the same. Keep your weight back through the heels to counteract the forward pull of the downswing, and remember that right elbow, which should brush by the right side trouser pocket on the downswing.

That old chestnut—the head—can also be responsible for heeling the ball. Head moving usually stems from another fault such as the forward rocking motion of the body (*see* SHANKING).

HIGH SHOTS: To raise the ball quickly, go for the underside, hitting ball and turf almost simultaneously. Position the ball up near the left toe so you'll catch it at the very end of your downswing arc.

Instead of closing the clubface by toeing in, open it a bit by toeing out, thus adding to its natural loft. See that your hands don't roll over and close the clubface before contact. Following my recommendation for slicing, complete your swing with the palm of your left hand down (*see* SLICE).

HOOK SHOT: The hook spin is from right to left. The clubface is closed (toed in), and you swing the clubhead around the ball from the inside out.

This stance and ball position will produce a high shot

Ball positioned nearer left toe with clubface opened a little

This is the hook swing. Note that the clubhead has traveled around the ball, exaggeratedly, from the inside out.

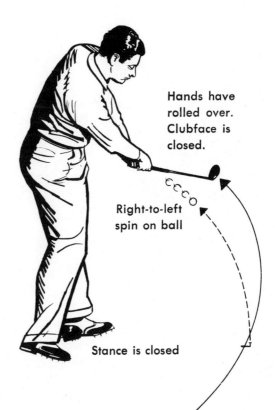

Hands have rolled over. Clubface is closed.

Right-to-left spin on ball

Stance is closed

To hook deliberately, place your right hand under the shaft; your left hand more on top of the shaft. The V's formed by the thumb and forefinger of each hand form a line pointing to the right shoulder.

In order to hit the ball from inside out, take the clubhead away on the inside.

Clubs of medium depth are best for hitting pronounced hooks. The 4-wood and the 4 and 5-iron are also great hook clubs.

CORRECTING THE HOOK

The hook is in all respects the opposite of the slice. The flight is different and so are the causes and cures.

The ball curves to the right when the clubface imparts a left-to-right spin. Put a right-to-left spin on the ball, and you get a left curve or hook.

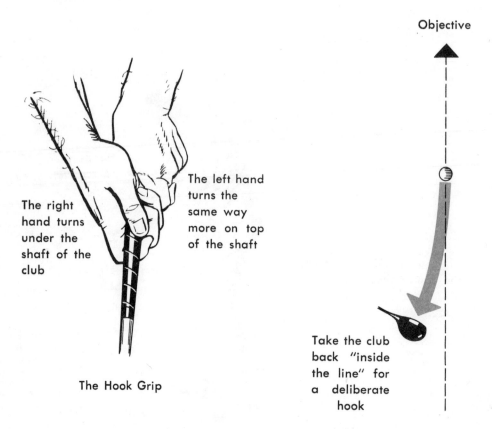

Objective

The right hand turns under the shaft of the club

The left hand turns the same way more on top of the shaft

The Hook Grip

Take the club back "inside the line" for a deliberate hook

Takeaway straight back

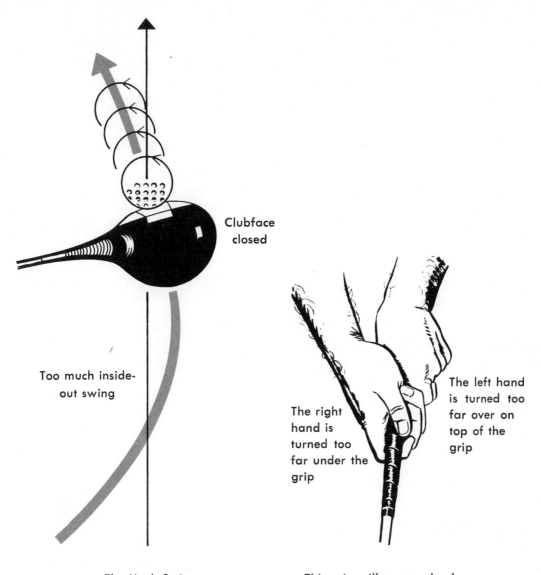

Clubface closed

Too much inside-out swing

The right hand is turned too far under the grip

The left hand is turned too far over on top of the grip

The Hook Swing

This grip will cause a hook

The right-to-left spin happens when the clubface is closed at impact, when the swing is too inside-out, or when both faults are combined, which is usually the case. If the term "inside-out" is confusing, think of a swing that's too much *around* the ball rather than cutting across it.

As with the slice, hook trouble is related to the grip. If the left hand is turned too far over to the right at the start, it will probably roll back over to the left on the downswing and you can count on a sweeping hook. And you can expect the same result if the right hand is too far to the right, or under the club.

If you are having trouble with a hook, check the grip. As explained in the GRIP section, when looking down at address, you should be able to see two knuckles of your left hand and one right hand knuckle.

If the grip is right, check the first movement of the backswing—the takeaway (*see* BACKSWING). If it is too much inside, you'll probably return along the same path and hook.

If the grip and takeaway are correct, you'd better investigate the position of the ball at address. If it is too far forward, you'll allow your hands too much room to turn over before the ball is met. Make this test, and you'll see that as the hands begin turning over, the clubface starts closing. The proper positioning of the ball for the drive is on a line with the left instep. That is as far forward as the ball should ever be positioned for a normal shot.

A chief cause of the quick hook—sometimes called the "ducking hook"—is trying to hit the ball from the top of the swing. This is the same as starting the hit too quickly. Remember that the start of the

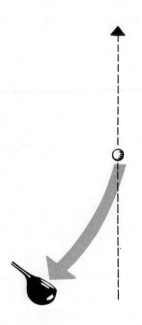

This takeaway is too much inside. It will cause a hook

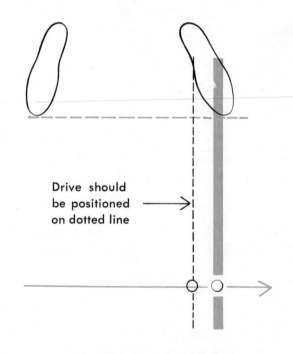

Drive should be positioned on dotted line

Incorrect: Ball positioned too far forward for driver

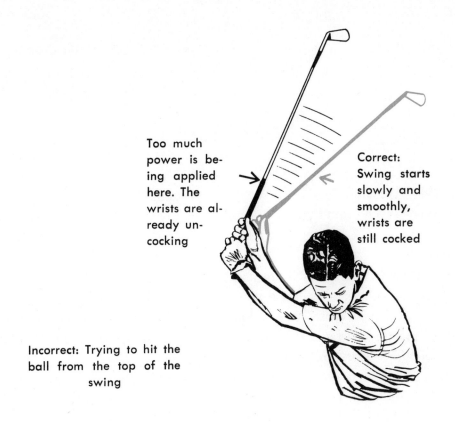

Too much power is be- ing applied here. The wrists are al- ready un- cocking

Correct: Swing starts slowly and smoothly, wrists are still cocked

Incorrect: Trying to hit the ball from the top of the swing

downswing must be slow and smooth. A number of serious errors result when you try to apply full power from the top. When you hit too quickly from the top your hands roll over before impact, and this error causes the hook.

I

IRONS: *See* CLUBS

J

JIGGERS: *See* CLUBS

L

LIE: Unusual lies are discussed in detail under DOWNHILL LIES, SIDEHILL LIES and UPHILL LIES. Sand lies are discussed in SAND TRAPS.

LOOKING UP: This is the catch-all fault of golf. "What did I do?" the duffer asks his fellow duffer after dribbling a shot along the ground for all of 20 yards. "You looked up," replies the fellow duffer, hardly giving the matter a thought. But he's probably right at that—looking up is the basic fault in many instances.

The fault is probably the simplest one in golf. When you look up, you've moved your head and the plane and focal point of your swing are out of kilter. You can't possibly meet the ball squarely.

You've also taken your eyes off the ball. Since muscular coordination depends on vision, you must keep your eyes fixed on the ball. It's as simple as that.

To overcome the fault of looking up (or moving your head), place your body at address so you *can* swing without moving your head (*see* ADDRESS TO THE BALL) and make up your mind in advance that you're going to keep your head still and your eyes on the ball.

LOOPING AT THE TOP: Looping the clubhead at the top of the swing is a needless complication of an operation that should be kept as simple as possible. Because the clubhead describes a loop or a circle at the top, the fault is also known as sky-writing.

Some golfers score well despite this looping at the top but most of them admit they'd do better without it.

In the simple, one-piece golf swing, you move your hands back to their best hitting position in one continuous movement and start down immediately from that position. The simplest way is really the

Determine in advance to keep the head still and the eyes on the ball

Changing position of hands at top of the backswing, causing a "loop" of the clubhead

most effective. By keeping the swing as simple as possible, it's easier to be consistent. After all, the ideal swing is the same action repeated over and over again without any changes or variations.

Looping the club at the top makes for general wildness. If you change the position of your hands when they are up in the air and out of sight, you never know just what they're doing.

LOW SHOTS: When you want to keep the ball low, position it back near the right foot—then you'll have to swing sharply down. Be sure you hit the ball before you take any turf; you don't want to come in underneath.

Your hands should be ahead of the clubhead. Toe in the clubface a bit to decrease its natural loft.

Hands ahead
of clubhead

Low shot   Turf taken after ball is hit

Hands rolled over

Ball should have been positioned here

Clubface closed

Incorrect: Ball positioned too far forward, causing a Skimmer

CORRECTING LOW SHOTS

The shot that skims a few feet or only a few inches above the ground —never as high as you want—is closely akin to the topped shot (*see* TOPPING).

This shot is distinguished from what is sometimes called the "cold top" in two ways: (*1*) It usually goes along at a uniform height for a few yards but hits the ground much too quickly, whereas the cold top drives the ball into the ground a few inches ahead of its original position, causing it to bounce up quickly and then roll a few yards at most. (*2*) The skimmer may result from a fault other than semi-topping, though this is usually the cause.

Aside from semi-topping, the clubface may close as the club meets the ball. This happens when you roll your hands over before impact.

This rolling action, which shuts the clubface almost completely, usually takes place when you position the ball too far forward. The hands should roll over during the swing to produce clubhead speed but only enough to bring the clubhead squarely into the ball with your hands in the same relative position as they were at address. This will happen if the ball is positioned properly so that the clubhead will meet it at the bottom of the swing arc. But if the ball is two inches in front of the bottom point, your hands are liable to turn over and shut that clubface tight. This does away with the club's natural loft.

The fault in question occurs most often with the driver or the 2-iron. These clubs are the least lofted of the standard set (putter excepted), and the least premature rolling of the hands will shut them entirely.

Another pernicious golf fault (the more you try to correct it, the worse it gets) is placing the ball ahead of the left toe. You might think that by doing this you can lift the ball more—and indeed, you can if you keep your hands from rolling over. But the farther forward you position the ball, the greater the chance that your hands will roll over before impact.

The answer here is proper positioning of the ball at address (*see* ADDRESS TO THE BALL).

As stated above, semi-topping causes most of the low liners when the bottom half of the clubface meets only the top half of the ball. With the less lofted clubs, this fault means an embarrassing loss of distance; with the more lofted clubs, you'll usually gain too much distance. On short chips or pitches, the fault is generally referred to as "blading" or "bellying" the shot. Instead of hitting the ball on its underside, you hit in the middle. The usual result is a screaming liner over the green or into an intervening bunker or the bank of the green.

The same faults responsible for the full top cause the half top, though to a lesser degree: straightning up, lifting the head, raising the right elbow above and outside the right hip, crooking the left elbow as you come into the ball.

The cures depend on maintaining the proper address position and still head, keeping the right elbow tucked in close with the left arm extended but not rigid, and hitting through the ball.

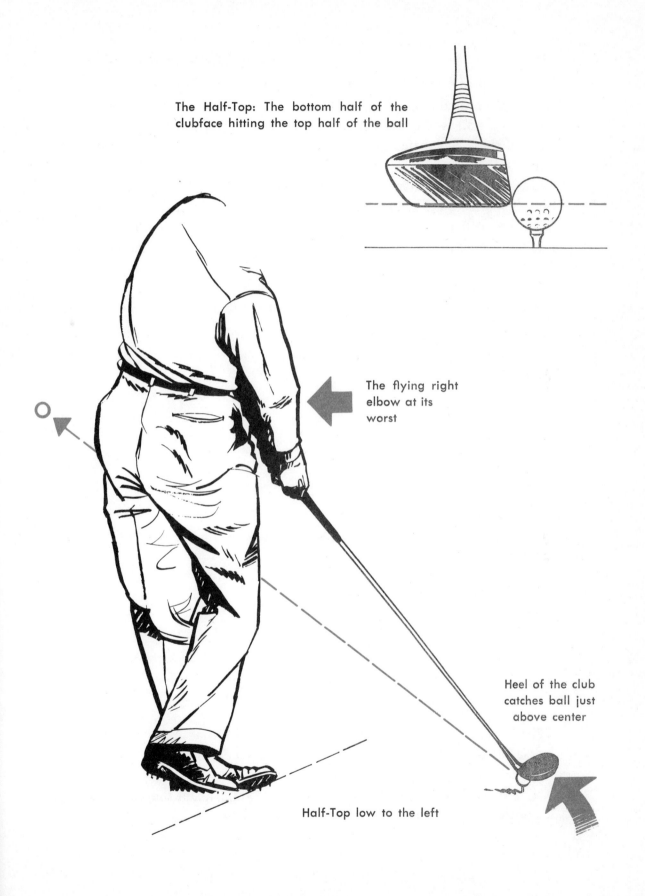

The Half-Top: The bottom half of the clubface hitting the top half of the ball

The flying right elbow at its worst

Heel of the club catches ball just above center

Half-Top low to the left

One kind of half-topped shot goes out under the left armpit—just the opposite of the shank. The shot looks very funny to your opponents, but you won't find the results so funny. You must have seen some of these shots—the ball sort of squirts out to the left and is very low.

The cause of this howler is the flying right elbow. It goes up and out; the plane of the swing does the same; the clubhead meets the ball from the outside in (as it must if you're going to hit the ball at all), and the heel of the club catches the ball just above center. As happens on the shank, the ball goes completely outside your line of vision so that you have to turn to the left to even see it. When this happens, you can be sure you're greatly exaggerating the flying right elbow.

M

MASHIE: *See* CLUBS

N

NIBLICK: *See* CLUBS

O

OFF-CENTER ERRORS: The group of golf errors that can generally be classified as "off-center errors" are shots in which the clubhead does not meet the ball squarely.

I agree with most golf theorists that one should teach the game in a positive manner just as it's played. But such is the nature of golf that you may lapse into a pattern of error and not know what to do about it. A lot of golfers hit the shank, for instance, without having the least idea why.

Building a sound golf swing is not a patchwork business of correcting faults wherever they may break out. The causes and cures of your errors overlap in many instances. The moving head is responsible for practically all errors; therefore, the stationary head helps keep most errors in check.

In some instances, one fault can be regarded as a variation of another—*i.e.*, shanking and hitting the ball in the heel of the club. That's why I've tried to isolate such errors cited in individual sections so that you can understand them more readily.

You can only play good golf if you swing the clubhead squarely into the ball. To achieve any consistency at all, you must estimate distance on the basis of square impact. It would be patently impossible to say, for instance, "I'm going to half top this shot, so I'll figure it in such a way that by half-topping, I'll send the ball about where it should go." Playing that way, you'll shoot about 200 for 18 holes, maybe more (*see* HEELING, HIGH SHOTS, HOOK, LOW SHOTS, SHANKING, SLICE, TOEING *and* TOPPING).

OVERSWINGING: This fault can result when your backswing is too long or when you try to "kill the ball."

The attempt to murder the ball is one of golf's most prevalent faults. It also poses one of golf's most perplexing questions: just how hard should a player try to swing at the ball? Controlled power is essential to good golf. On the other hand, you want to hit the ball as hard as you can. You've got to get it out there if your second shot is to be an easy one. And if you keep spotting the opposition yardage off the tee, you lower your chances of winning.

You should try to hit the ball with *all of the controlled power you have.* Give it the full treatment, I say, if you want the most accuracy for the greatest distance. I am convinced that the muscles work best when operating at full power. But if you try to add merely an ounce of extra power, you immediately try to "kill the ball."

You may have heard that champion sprinters try to "run relaxed" during the middle portion of a race. Otherwise, they lose some speed by trying too hard.

In his intense desire to hit the ball as far as he possibly can, the golfer is always tempted to try to hit it *harder* than he actually can. So he must make a conscious effort to "swing relaxed."

Now you won't be relaxed if you are trying to hit the ball hard. The needed muscle tension happens automatically. But you should make up your mind to swing hard in a relaxed manner. Nearly every golfer should guard against trying to swing harder than nature intended. Think of controlled power with emphasis on the word *controlled*.

SWING TOO LONG

As I've mentioned above, the overswing fault also includes the overlong swing. The player who takes the club too far back is nullifying his aim of swinging the clubhead squarely into the ball. He also loses some power because the farther back he swings, the less chance he gives himself to achieve maximum speed at contact.

We know that you must follow the hands and clubhead in your mind's eye once they pass beyond your line of vision on the backswing. When you take the club even farther back, you make this operation twice as difficult.

For a full drive, bring back the club to a point where the shaft is parallel with the ground and your hands slightly behind the right shoulder (*see* BACKSWING). You shorten the swing with the lesser clubs so that the backswing shortens as you change from driver to short irons.

Of course, a full backswing for one player may constitute a somewhat shorter swing for another golfer. But the maximum take-back point is the same in all cases—club shaft level and parallel with the ground.

My full drive backswing, which is shorter than most pros', stops just short of the point where the club shaft is level with the ground. But the difference is so slight as to be hardly noticeable.

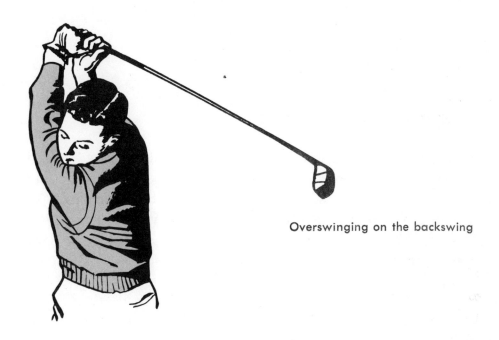

Overswinging on the backswing

My backswing for the Drive stops just short of the point where the club shaft is level with the ground.

P

PITCH SHOT: *See* SCORING RANGE

PITCHING WEDGE: I have separated the pitching wedge from the standard 2 through 9-iron set to emphasize the point that you seldom apply full power with this club. The full shot with the pitching wedge will normally go extremely high, which makes it difficult to control. You'd better hit a three-quarter or half shot with one of the short irons when the distance is roughly ninety yards—the most you can expect from the pitching wedge.

The club has a loft of about 55 degrees and is nearly an ounce heavier than the standard irons. You use it for pitches around the green when you want the ball to get up quickly and stop on a dime (*see* SCORING RANGE).

If you use the pitching wedge for a full shot, as is sometimes the case when you need a very high shot with a lot of underspin, play it with the same stroke you'd use for the 9-iron (*See also* CLUBS).

POOP SHOT: *See* SCORING RANGE

POSITIONING: *See* ADDRESS TO THE BALL *and* PUTTING

PSYCHOLOGY OF GOLF: My experience tells me that it's not enough to outline the correct tactics and insist that the student use them. Too often I've discovered that the player proceeds from the first tee with the best of intentions only to lose out through some unforeseen development.

Maybe he'll flub a short putt on one of the early holes and spend the rest of the round brooding about it. Or maybe an opponent will get a couple of lucky breaks that discourage our man to the extent that he can't think a problem through.

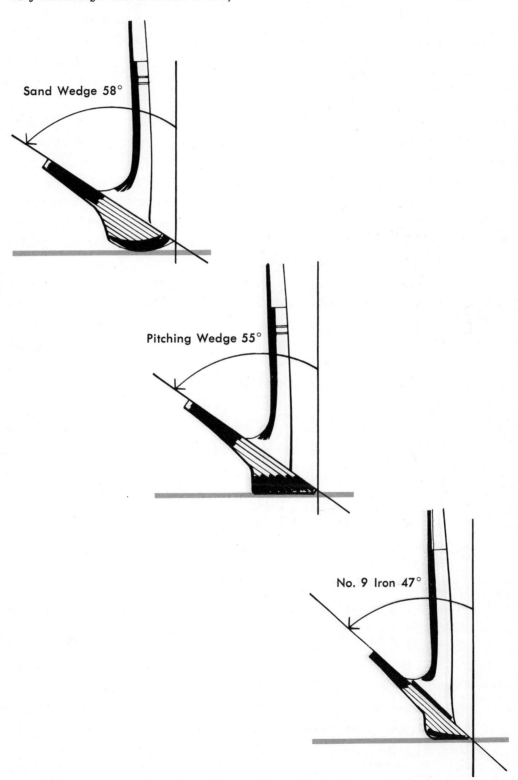

Sand Wedge 58°

Pitching Wedge 55°

No. 9 Iron 47°

The golfer who wants to become a good competitor must learn to develop a strategy for the whole round. He must realize from the start that he's going to miss a few easy shots and that his opponent will probably get a few breaks. You've got to keep playing your own game the way you've planned it.

Try to figure out how many simple mistakes you're likely to make in the course of a round and then make up your mind not to become discouraged before you've made them all. After all, some breaks will go against you, some for you, and the former may precede the latter. The good breaks will come your way if you stick to sound principles.

Some golfers tend to come up with a good shot in a pinch. Others seem doomed to frustrating failure whenever a golfing situation arises that calls for something special.

Say you are on the 18th green and you need a four-foot putt to win the match for your side. Forget about how you're going to feel if you miss the putt or even the kind words you can expect from your partner if you sink it. Concentrate on the putt—nothing more. Determine to hit the putt to the best of your ability, and let it go at that.

I need hardly add that the same attitude is a prerequisite for hitting the long ball.

Good golf requires sound thinking and a sound swing. Sound thinking on the golf course will save you a minimum of six shots per 18-hole round.

I think the estimate is a conservative one. The golfer who does not pay attention to the tactical side of golf is like a baseball pitcher who simply throws the ball as hard as he can in the hope that he can get it over some part of the plate.

In most other games, a player's strategy depends on what the other fellow is likely to do. This is somewhat true of golf strategy too, though the main opponent is really the golf course. If you play the course intelligently, you needn't worry about the opposition.

In order to understand the golfer's basic problem, let's investigate a basic situation wherein the strategy is quite simple though ignored by thousands of golfers to the detriment of their scores.

Assume that you are an average golfer—a 90 shooter who averages about one over par per hole. Being the average golfer, you make about six pars in the course of a round. Also, you make three or four double-bogeys (two over par on a single hole and probably one horrible score such as an eight or nine.

Now, if we can increase the number of your pars by one or two, cut down those double-bogeys by one or two and eliminate that one horror score then you'll have a score down in the middle or low 80's.

Okay, here's the situation. The hole is a par-four, 430 yards long. Your average drive is about 210 yards, and assuming a good lie, you can usually depend on 190 to 200 yards with a fairway wood. In other words, you've practically no chance of reaching the green in two shots.

Then here's the *key* to the proper strategy: your chance of a par on the hole *depends on a good third shot* followed by a one-putt. That's the way you should approach the problem, starting with the drive. Try to be safe and sure on the drive. No use trying to put something extra into your tee shot. No use flirting with danger at this point. Try to hit for your normal distance to reach a position for a normal second shot.

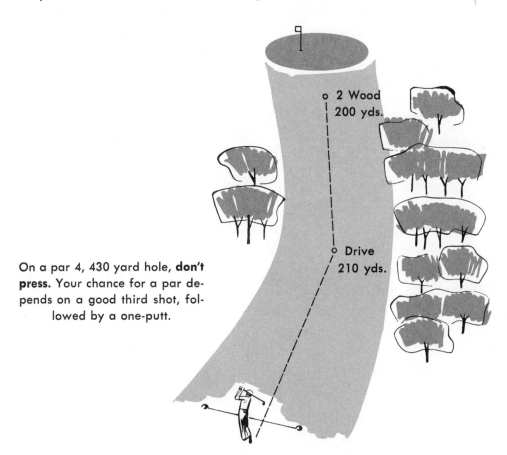

2 Wood
200 yds.

Drive
210 yds.

On a par 4, 430 yard hole, **don't press.** Your chance for a par depends on a good third shot, followed by a one-putt.

Play for the big part of the fairway, remembering that you want to be in position to make your *big move* on the third shot.

Safety is another important consideration on your second shot. If you have a nice lie on the fairway and think you *might* lift the ball up and away with a 2-wood, don't try it. Play the 3-wood for safety's sake. After all, five or ten yards' distance isn't going to matter much at this point. But if you try to get fancy on that second shot and flub it, you've killed your big chance for that par-making third shot. And for what? Nothing—nothing at all.

If you take care on the second shot, you'll more than likely end up some 20 yards away from the hole, shooting three. Then you'll have a good chance for a possible par. At worst, you should make a bogey. And that's the situation you were shooting for right from the start.

From 20 yards out, the average golfer can frequently match shots with the good golfer. The latter is usually superior with the long shots. In the situation we have set up, our average player has come a long way toward equalizing things. Very likely he'll make either a par or a bogey. Generally speaking, it will be the same with your 75-shooter— on a 430-yard hole, he'll figure to make par slightly more often than he'll bogey.

Note what would probably have happened had our player tried to slug his drive in the hope of reaching the green in two shots. Percentage-wise, he would have hit a wild drive or slammed the ball off center. Most certainly he would have obtained less distance than if he had tried to meet the ball nicely to be in position for a second shot.

As for his second shot, maybe he could have taken the two-wood and reached the green with a lucky shot. But probably not. And as we have seen, the second shot was *not* the one on which he wanted to stake his chances.

This is basic golf strategy for good, bad and average players. Even the top pros must learn to "get the pars and let the birdies come when they will." The good player should base his strategy on setting up pars. The average and below average players should base their strategy on setting up *possible* pars. That's the story in a nutshell.

Aside from your overall strategy prior to your first shot on a hole, many tactical situations arise while playing that hole. Say that your

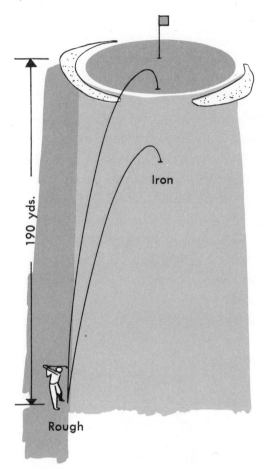

With your ball in the rough 190 yards from the green, it will usually be smarter to hit an iron into the fairway. If you should miss a 4 Wood shot, you might dribble the ball along a few yards and still be in the rough.

ball is in the rough about 190 yards from the green. You feel that *if* you can get the ball up and away with a four-wood, you *may* get it on the green. If not, you'll probably dribble the ball along for a few yards and still be in the rough.

Your alternative is to get the ball out of the rough with an iron to a point some yards short of the green. From there you may be able to pitch up close for a one-putt green. This is generally the preferable course. Note that you're now relying on the short pitch instead of the long shot from the rough. The key to the problem is to choose the most likely way of holing the ball in three shots from your position in the rough.

Go with your best chance, and you'll solve most of the tactical problems you'll encounter.

PULLED SHOT: The pull is the opposite of the push and differs from the hook in that the ball starts off and continues on a line left of the target, instead of curving. Body sway causes a lot of pulled shots. When you move back off the ball on the backswing and then stay behind it on the downswing, you are lined up to the left of the target.

Lazy footwork is also responsible for the pulled shot. The player swings flatfooted, so to speak, and fails to transfer his weight to the left side on the downswing. Result: a roundhouse swing that sends the ball off to the left.

Therefore, to avoid the pull, cut out the sway and pay attention to the footwork prescribed in STANCE. You raise your left heel enough for a full body turn and replace it quickly and decisively as the downswing begins so that it bears most of your weight. The right heel is pulled off the ground during the weight transfer to the left side.

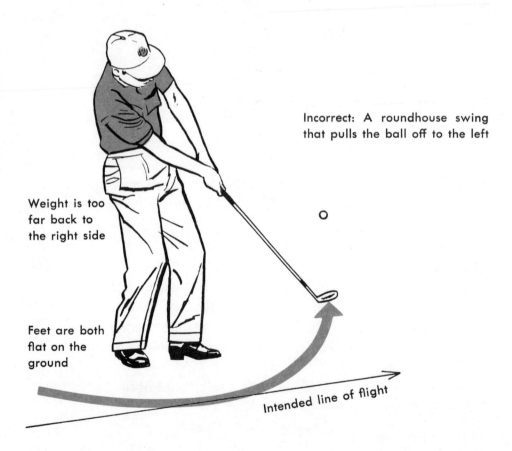

Incorrect: A roundhouse swing that pulls the ball off to the left

Weight is too far back to the right side

Feet are both flat on the ground

Intended line of flight

Club is lined up to the left of the target

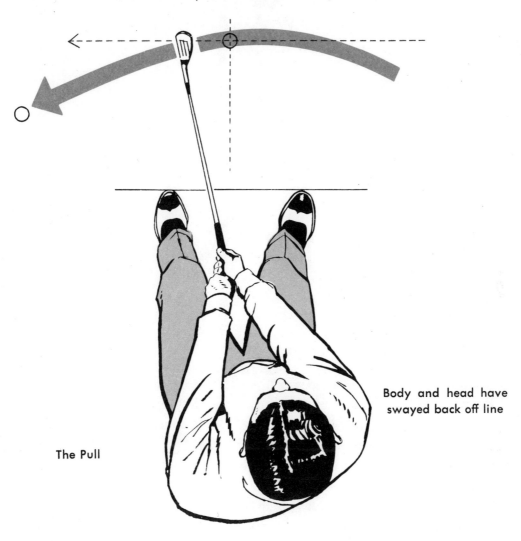

Body and head have
swayed back off line

The Pull

PUSHED SHOT: Like the slice, the push shot sends the ball to the right of the target. When you shift the alignment of your body with the intended direction of flight, you'll push the ball.

You sway your body and your head position changes so that you are actually lined up differently than you were at address. Sometimes you can compensate for the sway and hit a fairly straight ball. But when you sway on the backswing, you can rarely use the same amount of sway on the downswing, which is what must come about if you are

Body and head have
swayed back off line

to hit a straight ball. It is so much easier to turn the body around on
the backswing and then unwind during the downswing.

If you raise your left heel too far off the ground on the backswing
and then fail to replace it in exactly the same position on the downswing, you'll also push. The best idea is to raise the left heel just
enough for the required amount of body rotation. Then it's a safe
bet you'll replace it where it belongs.

To understand the left heel position, raise it high and then set it
down ahead of its position at the start of the swing. Note how you are
actually lined up to hit the ball many yards to the right of your
original goal.

It follows then that the cure for pushing the ball is to keep the head
in the same position throughout the swing and raise the left heel only
enough for a full body turn. In this case, "keeping the head still" means
more than "keeping the eye on the ball." It is possible, you see, to
keep your eye on the ball and still move your head. Think of your
head as the pivot around which the swing revolves.

Left heel is raised too far off the ground on the backswing

PUTTER: Since the overwhelming majority of your strokes per round will be putting strokes, it scarcely needs to be said that the most important club in your bag is your putter.

Selection of the putter that fits your game is a delicate affair of courtship and marriage: you are the only person alive who knows when you've found the right one; and, once you've made your choice, it will be the key to every round you play.

Three criteria that might be offered to help you in this selection are: (*1*) Shape of the head. (*2*) Shaft length. (*3*) Weight. Choose a putter shaped so that its head will rest squarely and comfortably on the ground with your eyes directly over the ball. The length of the shaft should be in accordance with your height; while the overall weight of your putter should be medium to heavy for use on both fast and slow greens.

As for the style of putter you choose, mallet-head or blade, individual preference is the only criterion. Like most playing professionals, I prefer the mallet-head putter; but many outstanding golfers have been successful with the blade instrument. What counts is to find the putter that *feels* right for *you*.

PUTTING: On occasion I have been called "the world's greatest putter." I remember that a kindly magazine writer once bestowed that enviable title on me. And I have been given that title—temporarily—by opponents who caught me on one of those too-rare days when everything happened to be dropping.

There have been other occasions when I knew without anybody having to tell me that I was the world's worst putter. As the saying goes, I just couldn't buy a putt.

But whether I putt well or badly, the fact remains that for many years now I have studied the putting styles of all the many good putters I have seen, and I have tested every putting theory that has come my way. As a result of these studies and tests, I've concluded that (1) there are certain principles on which most good putting is based and (2) some good putters defy at least one of these principles. Conversely, there are golfers who seem to putt with a stroke that embodies all the correct principles and seldom hole a putt of any size. In other words, putting is largely an individual matter, but if you follow certain rules, you'll have a *better chance* to become a good putter.

I wish to emphasize early in this section that I am not advocating that any golfer who already putts well should alter his style. Far from it! I believe that all good putters should stick to their own style.

I am convinced, however, that all golfers who have putting troubles (and that includes most of us) should understand that a good putting stroke is basically similar to a good stroke for other shots. You take the club straight back, meet the ball squarely and continue straight for several inches. The golfer who departs from these basic principles may putt well at times but he won't be consistent.

Consistency is the aim of your putting stroke. Once you've developed a stroke that places the head of the putter in solid contact square to the line of flight, you can give more attention to such considerations as the speed of the green, the amount of break to play, etc.

APPROACH PUTTS

The object of the approach putt is to get the ball close enough to the hole to make the next putt a simple tap-in. The big problem is determining how hard to hit the ball.

Try to make your putt fall in the hole at the last turn of the ball. In other words, the best way to achieve near-perfection (getting the ball close to the hole) is to strive for perfection (holing the ball).

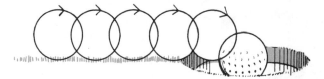

Approach putting: Try to make
the ball fall in the hole on its
last turn

You've probably heard about the magic circle theory whereby you try to make the ball stop within an imaginary circle whose radius is three feet from the hole. To my mind, this is the negative approach in which your goal is near-perfection. Why not aim at perfection?

Study your long putts one step at a time. First, study the green for the likely speed of your putt. *Before* you assume your putting stance you must judge such conditions as the length, texture and grain of the grass, the amount of break (if any) and the grade, whether uphill, downhill or level.

Imagine the ball following the proper line and losing its last bit of momentum at the very lip of the cup, so that the last turn carries it over the front edge of the cup. Your sense of touch determines the amount of power you apply to the stroke to make the ball reach the hole and not overshoot it. Only you can judge the power you require. No one can say that for a 50-foot putt you should take back the putter so many inches and swing forward so hard.

Aside from sizing up the lay of the land and exercising a sure touch, you should be sure that you hit the ball solidly on the putter face. Finally, approach putting calls for a positive mental attitude free of any "ifs" and "buts."

MIDDLE-RANGE PUTTS

The middle range of putting includes putts ranging from 12 to 20 feet. If you can hole three or four of these in the course of a round, you can cut down your score and raise hob with the opposition. Unless you are a wizard on the greens, you won't often hole three or four of these babies in a single round, but you can hole more than your normal share.

Lining up my last putt on the 18th green at the Inverness Club. I managed to sink this 10 foot putt to tie Dick Mayer for the 1957 Open.

According to my experience, most players pay too little attention to the possibility of *making* these middle-range putts. They try to get close, not in. Why? Well, even the best putters can expect to hole only one out of five of these putts, a discouraging business for the average duffer, who then makes only a half-hearted effort.

Perfection is the goal for long and short putts. As for the middle-range putts, I feel that if the player really gives them his best try at all times, he'll hole his fair share. His fair share may be only one in five, or less, depending on his ability. But if he doesn't really level on these middle-range putts and settles for getting in close, he'll hardly ever hole a putt of any appreciable length. This is the difference between a good putter and an average or poor one.

When you are faced with a 15-footer, sight along the line you expect the ball to take. Imagine the ball following that line and plopping into the cup just before it runs out of momentum. Always think of a successful putt. A lot of them—most, in fact—will miss even with your best effort. But some will go in.

SHORTER PUTTS

I believe that most poor putts of 4 to 8 feet stem from too much care and effort. This is an opposite situation from the one discussed in the middle-range section. I realize that this is an arbitrary distinction that does not apply in every case. But according to my experience, I believe it applies in most cases.

The average player feels he *must* make these fairly short putts. It shakes him to think of adding two full strokes to his score for negotiating a distance of little more than a yard—perhaps the same number of strokes it took him to reach the green. Quite often this short putt determines whether the player makes his par or settles for a bogey. The par usually means success on the hole, the bogey failure. Or you may be putting for a much-desired birdie, a more tense situation. Whatever score the putt represents, it is usually very important to the player.

On very short putts, be careful, but be firm

You can make most of these putts if you concentrate on the business at hand—making the putt. Sight in on the line without too much fuss and bother. Picture the ball following this line, passing over the front lip of the cup and dropping in. Stroke the putt with all the confidence you can muster. Don't let the importance of the shot cause you to tense up.

No one makes all his putts from this range. Fifty per cent is a pretty good average from the 6 to 8-foot range. From 4 feet, you should probably sink approximately three-fourths. Hit these putts as best you can so you'll get your share. Don't tense up. Don't think yourself out of these putts by fooling around with them too long.

VERY SHORT PUTTS

On little putts of two feet and less the golfer should be careful but not *too* careful. The player misses most of these shorties through an excess of care as well as carelessness.

The reason for careless misses is obvious. The player thinks his little putt is a cinch. So he walks up and taps it without thought or aim. This will work most of the time, but sooner or later it will cost you strokes. The ball will slide by the cup, and you'll be talking to yourself all the way back to the club house.

On the other hand, if you give too much time and thought to a very short putt, you'll tense up. Don't make a production of what is after all a simple operation.

BALL POSITION

If you can develop a "repeating" stroke in which each putt follows the same basic pattern, your practice sessions will become much more profitable.

On straight and level putts, always position the ball the same way. Then from this key positioning, you can make slight alterations for downhill, uphill, right and left-breaking putts. And your putting pattern won't change.

With very few exceptions, the better putters position the ball for a straight and level putt just inside the left toe or close to it. Some fine putters position the ball exactly opposite the center of the left toe.

Position the ball for a straight and level putt just inside the left toe

Others line up the ball off the left heel. The degrees of variation are insignificant.

When you line up the ball well forward, you can sight along the intended line of flight much more easily. Moreover, you'll contact the ball at the end of the arc instead of hitting down on it for an underspin. The ball that rolls straight with no spin will hew to the line and plop into the cup more readily. And forward positioning makes for a steady roll with no "English."

But putting is not an exact science. And while I favor the forward positioning, some of you may find it more helpful to adopt another position, with the ball nearer the center of the feet, for instance. In any event, stick to your basic pattern once you've found it.

Downhill putts: When you assume your stance for a downhill putt, your left foot will be slightly lower than your right. If you were to maintain the same positioning you use for a straight and level putt, the end of your swing arc would be different. This change would also take place for a regular shot from a downhill lie.

You only need alter your position slightly. Stand so that the ball is about a half inch nearer the right foot. This adjustment will place the ball in the same position you would use for the straight and level putt. You compensate for the uneven terrain in order to keep your basic putting pattern the same.

Uphill putts: For an uphill putt, simply alter the basic level position in the opposite manner from the downhill putt adjustment. Position the ball a little more forward. Then the arc of your swing will follow the same pattern you use for a level putt.

Right-breaking putts: Line up a right-breaking putt with a point to the left of the hole. So you should position the ball a little farther forward than you would for a level putt.

You should stand somewhat closer to the ball on a putt that breaks right because you will be standing slightly above the ball.

Left-breaking putts: For putts that break left, simply reverse the pattern for the right-breaking jobs. Position the ball farther back and stand back more.

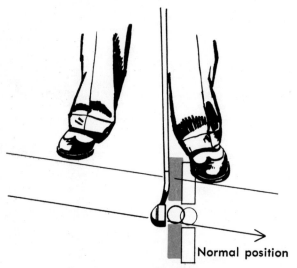

Stand so that ball is moved back a half inch nearer the right foot for a downhill putt

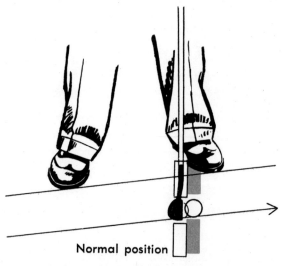

Position the ball a little forward for an uphill putt

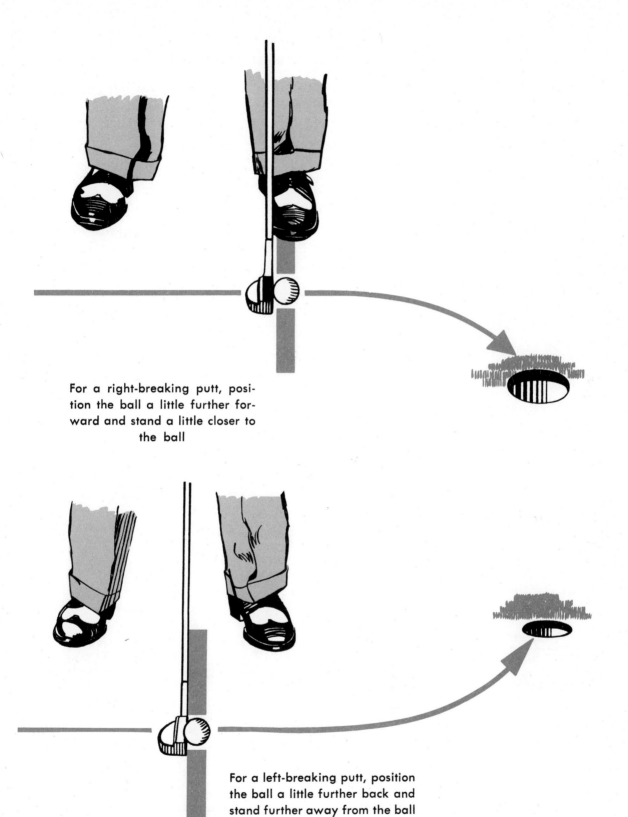

For a right-breaking putt, position the ball a little further forward and stand a little closer to the ball

For a left-breaking putt, position the ball a little further back and stand further away from the ball

GRIP

Pressure and hand position are of first importance to the putting grip.

Most good golfers use a hand position in which both thumbs point straight down the shaft and the left index finger overlaps the fingers of the right hand much as the little finger of the right hand overlaps in the standard grip. There are a number of minor variations to this "reverse overlapping grip" some of which are better suited to individual needs.

If your hands are to work as a unit, they should *oppose each other* as much as possible on the shaft. The back of the left hand and the palm of the right should face the hole.

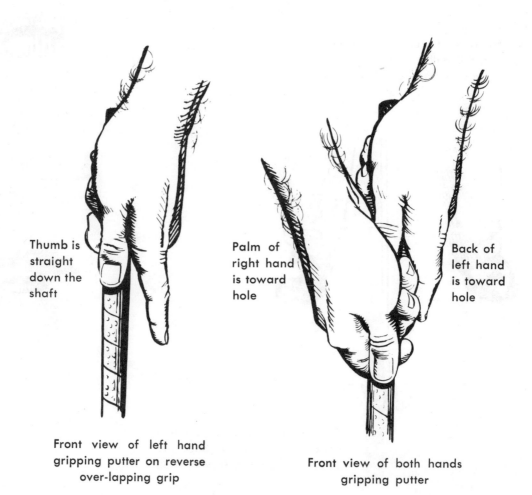

Thumb is straight down the shaft

Palm of right hand is toward hole

Back of left hand is toward hole

Front view of left hand gripping putter on reverse over-lapping grip

Front view of both hands gripping putter

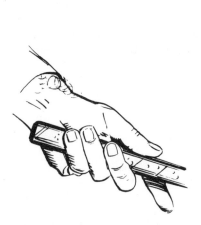

Side view of putter grip
for left hand

Incorrect: Choking up on
putter for short putts

Since putting requires a delicate and sensitive touch, the grip is all in the fingers. Some golfers grip the end of the shaft for long putts and choke down on the shaft for short ones. You can't be consistent this way. All putting strokes should be alike in simplicity of execution, excepting, of course, the amount of pressure you apply in each instance.

The putting grip differs radically from the standard grip in the use of power. You simply take the putter back a few inches—seldom more than 24 inches—and return it along the same straight line square to the ball and line of flight.

Pressure: The pressure you apply in the putting grip is of greater relative importance than the position of the hands. According to my observation, most golfers grip the putter too loosely while others hold it too firmly and tensely for accurate putting. Your grip must be steady enough to prevent turning of the clubhead, yet delicate enough for a sensitive touch.

Take the putter back a few inches straight along a line away from the ball, then bring it back along the same line

Hold your putter gently but firmly. If you grip it too loosely, you'll grab the putter again during the stroke and miss your putt. You can avoid this hitch if you grip the putter firmly to begin with and maintain a steady pressure throughout the stroke. Never change the pressure of the grip once you begin the stroke.

LINING AND SIZING UP PUTTS

Follow one step at a time in executing a putt. The first major step is to decide just what it is that you intend to do. You should know how hard you must hit the ball to reach the hole and how much, if any, the ball will veer from a straight course on its way to the hole.

In other words, you should know how to read the green, always the mark of a superior putter. This reading ability is of no great importance to the player who continually plays the same course or the same few courses; once he knows the greens, he won't have to read them. But the player who plays a number of different golf courses, particularly ones in different sections of the country, will have to learn to read greens if he is to become a good putter.

The length, thickness and texture of the grass, its wetness or dryness and level (uphill or down) determine the speed of the green. Another subtle factor is the *grain*, which like the grain in a piece of wood indicates the direction of growth. Putting a ball against the grain of a green is analogous to planing a piece of wood against the grain. But while a wood grain is clearly visible, the grain of a green is often difficult to determine.

The best way to determine grain on a green is to look for shine. When you're studying the hole and the green presents a sort of glazed or shiny surface, you know your putt is going with the grain and the ball will roll a lot more freely and much farther than you might suppose upon a more cursory investigation. Conversely, if the surface of the green presents a dull appearance, then you're looking against the grain, and you must hit the ball much harder than you'd think at first glance.

Bent grass greens of the type generally found in the North and East are usually very grainy. (This is especially true if there are mountains nearby since grass tends to grow away from the mountains in the direction of water.) Bermuda greens, such as are found throughout the South, usually have a more consistent grain. In fact, most of the grain found in Bermuda grass greens is the result of cutting in one direction. At any rate, the shine test is the most effective for Bermuda or bent.

The grain affects the speed of a putt and the direction in which it rolls. Let's say that the green slants just slightly to the left but the

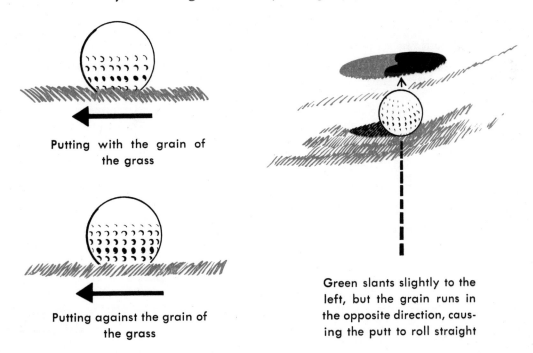

Putting with the grain of
the grass

Putting against the grain of
the grass

Green slants slightly to the
left, but the grain runs in
the opposite direction, causing the putt to roll straight

grain runs in the opposite direction. In this case you should hit the putt directly at the hole because the grain offsets the slight slant of the green. In any event, the grain will affect the amount of break you should play—something you'll have to determine when you line up the putt and don your thinking cap.

The first consideration in reading a green is to judge the speed with which the ball is likely to roll. Pay particular attention to the grass and the contour of the green within a three-foot radius of the hole. If the grass near the hole is comparatively heavy or if the putt must travel uphill the last few feet, go fairly strongly for the hole. You see, you won't need to worry as to what the ball will do if it gets past the hole.

Uphill roll near cup in
heavy grass

This putt had to be hit strongly

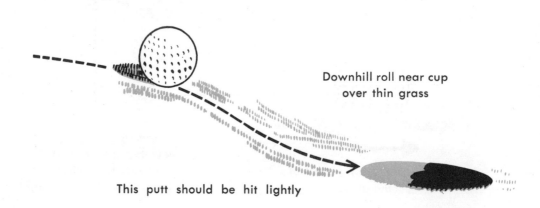

Downhill roll near cup
over thin grass

This putt should be hit lightly

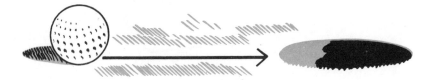

Putting against grain—Be bold

Putting with grain—Use caution

On the other hand, if the grass immediately surrounding the hole is thin or the last part of the putt is downhill, you should be extremely cautious. You may have to hole the following putt. You can be bold when you putt against the grain; when you putt with it, take care.

Once they've seen the first putt overshoot the mark, many players are somewhat timid on return putts. A little nerve will go a long way in such a situation. For one thing, you can usually find a good line on these return putts. When it rolls by, the ball naturally follows the line of least resistance in coming to a stop, and it will generally follow the same line on the return putt. So sight along the line the ball took when it rolled past the hole, make a very slight adjustment for error and stroke the putt with confidence. Where you are putting *with the grain* and the ball slides by a few feet, you'll be returning *against the grain.* If you don't consider this difference on the return putt, you'll probably lose your nerve and fall short.

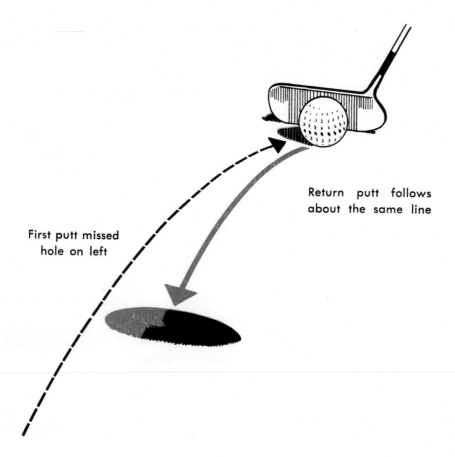

Return putt follows
about the same line

First putt missed
hole on left

STANCE

The putting stance should be comfortable and free of tension. Your eyes should be directly over the ball.

In my opinion, your feet should be two to eight inches apart. They must be slightly apart if you're going to keep your balance. Also, if they're too close together, your shoulder muscles may bunch up. Don't place your feet too far apart or you'll lock your knee joints and stiffen your leg muscles.

Many good putters use a very narrow stance. Others use a stance as wide as their shoulders. A few good putters keep their feet together; some even spread their feet wider than the breadth of their shoulders. Latter instances are exceptions that succeed in spite of the stance.

Correct Putting Stance

Eyes directly over ball

Correct Putting Stance — F e e t comfortably apart to maintain balance

Open, closed or square? Some players favor an open putting stance (right foot ahead of the left). They claim that by partially facing the hole, they improve their aim.

Others—including Bobby Locke, one of the best—favor a closed putting stance (right foot behind the left). They say they can take back the putter slightly inside the line so that their downswing will impart an overspin to the ball.

I favor a square stance, toes parallel to the line, because it enables me to putt square to the ball.

Body position: Be comfortable. Don't be tense. Keep your eyes directly over the ball. Flex your knees. Use the semi-sitting position advocated for regular shots. In that way you can relax and your hips won't be in the way of your elbows.

Keep a straight back, bending your head from the neck only. The crouch is detrimental to putting because it makes you tense and keeps your eyes ahead of the ball instead of directly over it.

Weight distribution: I feel that your weight should be evenly distributed over both heels. Some successful putters begin their stroke with most of their weight on the left foot. However, this positioning

Incorrect: Feet
too far apart

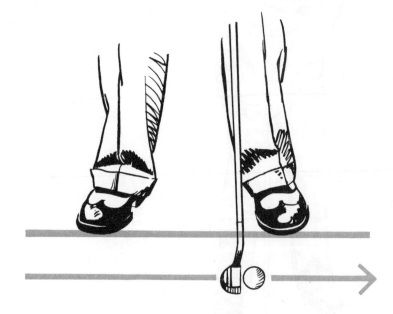

Square putting stance

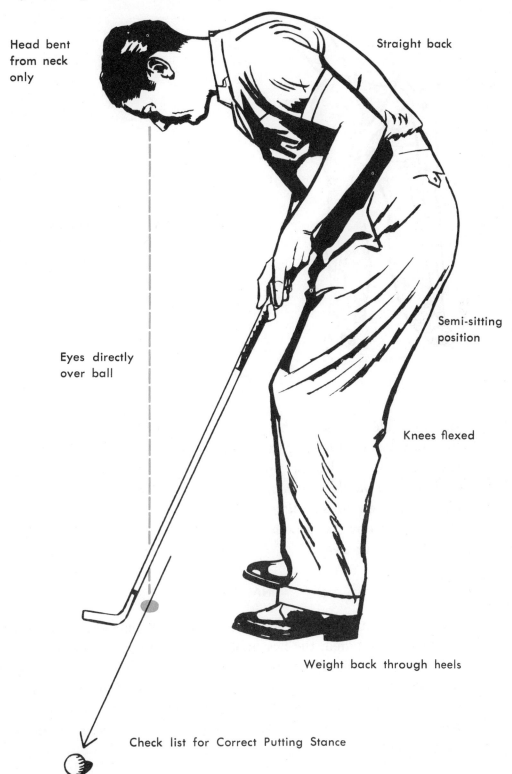

Head bent from neck only

Straight back

Eyes directly over ball

Semi-sitting position

Knees flexed

Weight back through heels

Check list for Correct Putting Stance

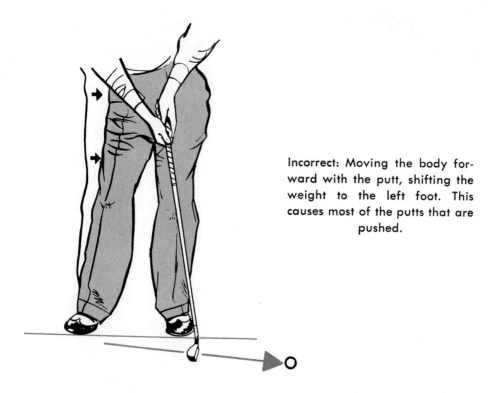

Incorrect: Moving the body forward with the putt, shifting the weight to the left foot. This causes most of the putts that are pushed.

is responsible for one of the most frequent of putting errors, moving the body toward the hole at impact. Most of the pushed putts you see are caused by this forward movement.

How close should you stand? When you look down on a spot ahead of the ball, you are standing too close to the ball. Conversely, if you look straight down at a point between the ball and your feet, you're standing too far away.

FINAL SIGHTING

According to my own experience and that of some excellent putters whom I've consulted, the best method of sighting over the putt is to look along the proper line and *picture the ball following that line into the hole.* Imagine the ball rolling at the right speed at various stages of the putt. Let your eyes follow the line at the speed you want the ball to travel so that you'll get a longer and closer look at the line near the hole.

In other words, you should try to picture the perfect putt. Imagine the ball reaching the hole at a speed slow enough to fall in but fast enough so that it won't stop short. Then rivet your eyes on the spot in back of the ball where you'll be making contact.

You'll find that if you contact the ball solidly on each stroke, you won't leave it short of the cup. Nearly all putts that stop short are caused by an off-center stroke rather than a failure to swing hard enough.

Rivet your eyes on the back of the ball until it is struck and on its way

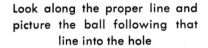

Look along the proper line and picture the ball following that line into the hole

Always glance quickly and decisively from the line you intend to follow to the back of the ball and keep your eyes glued there until you've made the putt.

THE TIME YOU TAKE

How much time should a player take standing over a putt? On the highest championship level of the game, Jimmy Demaret putts very quickly and Ben Hogan with great deliberation. Both are excellent putters, so we can only conclude that the amount of time you take depends on your temperament.

I have gone into considerable detail on lining up putts. While I recommend that you be careful and precise, don't take too *much* time.

Some players benefit from a long and thorough examination of the terrain between ball and hole. Most players do not. All the players I've watched fool around too long with their putts. You begin to figure out ways in which you can miss the putt instead of concentrating on sinking it.

Some putts require considerable study because of the subtle character of the break or the grain. Others are simple and should be stroked with a minimum of fuss and delay.

When sizing up a putt, your first impression is likely to be your best. In any event, you don't want two different impressions about the same putt. That makes for confusion.

Take it one step at a time. Judge the likely speed. Get the line. Decide how much force you need. Then walk up and knock it in. Be positive. Don't talk yourself out of a putt on which you've decided.

A great many "certain" putts are missed because the player stands over the ball too long. When you remain immobile in a position such as the putting stance for more than a few seconds, your muscles will surely tense up or cramp. And it's almost impossible to putt accurately under these circumstances. Yet you must aim carefully from a well adjusted stance.

What's the answer? That's for you to decide, though I suggest that as you practice putting, you study the amount of time you take with each putt. Try to determine your best time pattern and then stick with it.

MENTAL ATTITUDE

The whole putting process—lining up the shot, sighting and then hitting the ball—depends on your positive attitude toward play making. I know from experience that (1) bad putting often stems from the wrong kind of thinking and (2) you can control your thinking on the putting green.

If you let your mind dwell on the various possibilities of missing such as playing for too much or too little break, leaving the ball short, hitting it too hard, etc., you're setting up a miss. Think of the way you're going to *make* the putt. That's all that should interest you; nothing else should count.

Don't anticipate a miss or the problem posed by a miss. ("If I miss this one, I'll have another bogey on the card. I'll go another hole down! I'll never have a better chance to birdie this hole so I mustn't miss now!")

Always say to yourself, "I'm going to hit this putt along this line, and I intend to make it. I don't care what happens afterward—I'll look into that later."

BREAK

The contour and texture of the green, the grain of the grass, the force of your stroke and the distance of the shot determine the amount of break on your putt.

In most instances, you can see the slant of the green well enough to judge the break. When you're unable to determine the slant, the best solution is to examine the cup itself. If one side looks lower than the other, then the green *does* slant toward that side. Sometimes you can decide on the break by getting well away from the ball and taking a long-range look at the whole green area.

Once you've made up your mind that a break exists, then you should decide the amount of break and stick by your estimate.

As was pointed out earlier in this chapter, the grain of the grass

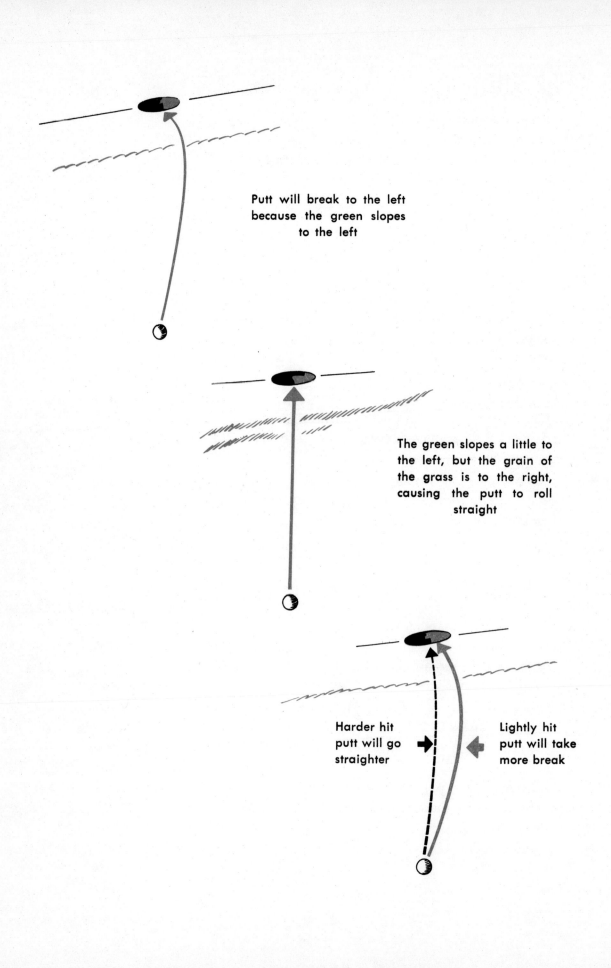

Putt will break to the left
because the green slopes
to the left

The green slopes a little to
the left, but the grain of
the grass is to the right,
causing the putt to roll
straight

Harder hit
putt will go
straighter

Lightly hit
putt will take
more break

affects the putt's break as well as its speed. Rolling speed is the important consideration when you are putting with or against the grain. But when you're putting across the grain, the break is all important. The shine test is effective in both cases. If you think there's enough grain to affect the break, examine the grain from the side. If there's a glaze or shine to the left of the cup, the break will be to the right, and vice versa. But unless the grain is very heavy, the effect on the break will be slight.

Force vs. break: Break depends a great deal on the force behind the putt. Of course, if the ball is travelling quite slowly, it will follow whatever break there is in the green. On the other hand, if it's moving briskly, its momentum will keep it more in line.

When the green is fast and you want to make the next putt if you miss this one, play the full apparent break, *i.e.*, let the ball reach the hole travelling quite slowly. But if the green is slow or you're in a match-play situation in which you'll lose the hole *anyway* unless you sink this putt, you can risk a firmer stroke to make the ball hew to the line.

This problem of force vs. break arises when you're not certain whether the ball will take a slight break or travel directly to the hole. If you decide to play the break, use only enough force to carry the ball over the front lip of the cup. Then if there's a slight break, the ball will take it. Conversely, if you decide to play the ball directly, you should hit it rather firmly. In that way, it will hold its line against a slight break that's not obvious.

Distance vs. break: The greater the distance a ball rolls along a slanted green, the more it will veer in the direction of the slant. But can we assume that the ball will roll at the same speed all the way along the slant and that it will break twice as far on a 24-foot putt as it will on a 12-foot putt?

No, because the ball does not maintain the same speed on a putt so that the break isn't consistent. In the early stages of the putt, the ball will be travelling with greater force and hence will tend to stay in line. The sharper break begins when the ball nears the hole and begins to roll more slowly.

This may be common sense, but you'd be surprised by the number of golfers who fail to take it into account when lining up a putt.

The green may show a sharp break for the first few feet and then level out as the ball nears the hole. Under such conditions, the tendency is to attach too much importance to the early break; the player allows for too much break and leaves the ball above the cup. The proper approach is to minimize the early break because the ball will have greater momentum in the early stages and will hold more closely to a straight line.

When the sharper break is near the hole, allow for the maximum break.

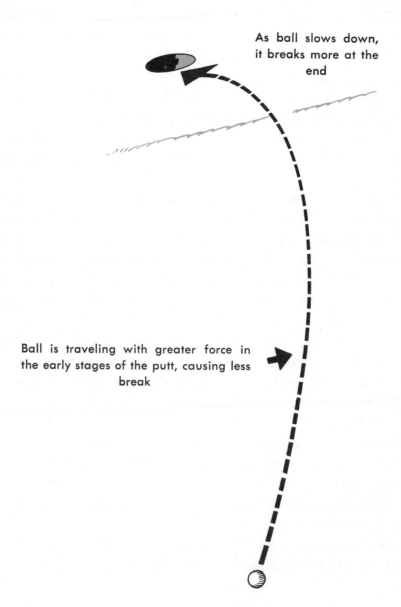

As ball slows down, it breaks more at the end

Ball is traveling with greater force in the early stages of the putt, causing less break

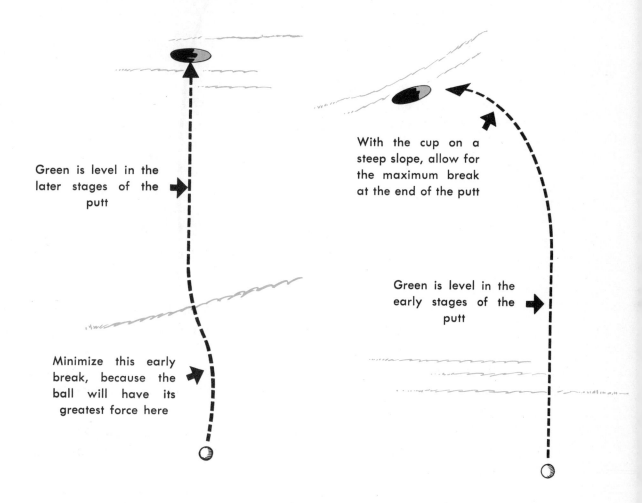

With the cup on a steep slope, allow for the maximum break at the end of the putt

Green is level in the later stages of the putt

Green is level in the early stages of the putt

Minimize this early break, because the ball will have its greatest force here

If the break is not consistent between the stroke and the cup, always check to determine where it lies. And when it is consistent, remember that the ball will not take the break as sharply in the early stages of the putt.

You will notice that most good putters closely examine the final three or four feet before the hole because that's when the ball will be most affected by any contour in the green.

Break and green texture: The final consideration in estimating the break on a given putt is the texture of the grass. If the green's texture

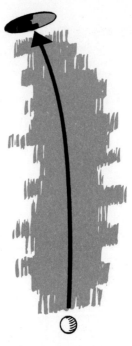

If the green is soft, and the grass is soft and pliable, the ball will travel more through the grass, causing less break

is such that the ball will roll through the grass, the break will be less than it would be if the ball were to roll along on top of the grass. If the green is soft and the grass soft and pliable, the ball will run through the grass and there'll be less break. If the green is hard, the ball will skim along the top of the grass, and take the full break as it appears.

When the green is wet, the ball tends to run through the moist grass. When the green is saturated with water, you can count on a minimum of break.

Summary: Once you have decided on the amount of break you can expect, stick by your decision. Never alter your plan in the act of putting.

There will be times when you miss a putt by misjudging the amount of break for which you should allow. But on many occasions your estimate will be correct, and you'll make it. With a wishy-washy attitude, however, you won't make any of these breaking putts.

Remember too to line up your putt according to the amount of break you expect. Don't depend on a deliberate pull or push of the putt to compensate for the break. This is a frequent putting fault.

If you think a putt will break one foot, pick out a spot one foot to the side of the hole in the opposite direction from the break. Line up on that spot.

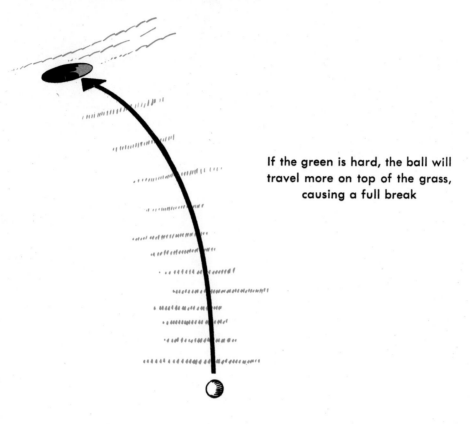

If the green is hard, the ball will travel more on top of the grass, causing a full break

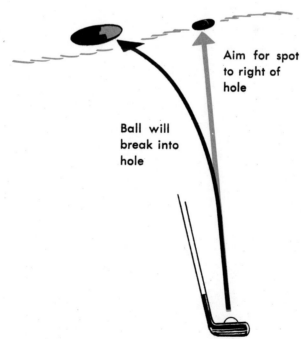

Aim for spot to right of hole

Ball will break into hole

The Waggle

WAGGLE

The actual putt begins with the waggle, which loosens the muscles and picks up the "beat" of your stroke while you're adjusting your line up.

The putting waggle should serve the same purpose it does for the full stroke. Don't fidget, but waggle in line with the intended stroke, schooling your muscles to execute the swing smoothly and directly.

The majority of golfers start the waggle with the putter in front of the ball. Theoretically, this is supposed to help them sight in, and by picking up the putter and placing it behind the ball, they can get their stroke smoothly under way. I seldom use the gimmick myself, though I can see no real objection to it. A great many very good putters use it (*see* WAGGLE).

BACKSWING

Swing back the putter in a smooth, unified action. For a time, the golfing world thought that the left hand should predominate in the putting backswing while the right hand commandeered the down-swing. This theory failed to hold up. The question as to which hand should dominate which swing led to too much pushing and pulling of putts. Actually the left hand plays the dominant role in the back-swing, the right hand in the downswing. But you should let the dominant hands take over naturally. Simply try to take the putter back smoothly in a straight line away from the ball and let your hands do what they have to do.

The backswing has to be smooth and cohesive—all of a piece. It can't be mechanical or contrived. Don't worry about the length of the backswing. Let the putter go *as far back as your sense of touch tells you it should go*. Don't consciously shorten your backswing or you'll jab the putt. And don't lengthen it either or you'll ruin your timing.

Here are two rules to remember:

Keep (*1*) the clubhead low along the ground and (*2*) the face of the putter square with the intended line of flight. The former rule

Correct putting backswing:
1. Keep clubhead low along ground
2. Keep the face of the putter square to the line of the putt
3. Slow backswing down

is important because you want the stroke to be a sweep rather than an up-and-down stroke. If you pick up the putter sharply on the backswing, you'll be forced to hit down on the ball.

The face of the putter should be square to the line of flight, since that's the way it should be at impact. If you open or close the face on the backswing, you'll only have to readjust somewhere along the line. And this is a difficult adjustment.

Speed: The speed of the backswing is a matter of individual taste. Some very effective putters use a brisk backswing; others are quite deliberate in their action.

However, I've found that the majority of golfers tend to bring the putter back too fast just as they do with the other clubs. Make a conscious effort to slow down your action so that it will be smooth. The more important the putt, the greater the tendency to swing back too fast. If the player feels he *has* to get a putt in, he's likely to speed up the swing "to get the darn thing over with." He may be quite deliberate in his preparations, but once over the ball, he becomes anxious.

To pause or not to pause? I've studied putting assiduously for many years and have reached a number of conclusions as to what

Brief pause at the end
of the backswing

works best for *most* players. I've found that a brief pause at the end of the backswing will help make you a better putter by enabling you to execute a smooth transition from backswing to downswing. I believe that most putting strokes go awry during this transition. Anxiety is most often the culprit.

What is more natural than to become anxious in the middle of a putt? You're so concerned about the delicate operation you're performing that you hasten into the downswing before the backswing is completed. This makes for jerky action and missed putts.

A brief pause is the best method of separating the backswing from the downswing. Make it very brief, but remember that you must complete the backswing before you start the downswing.

DOWNSWING

For a smooth downswing, start slowly. The clubhead should accelerate gradually as it moves toward the ball. Keep the head of the putter square with the line of flight.

The slow start of the downswing is the most important thing to remember. Try it first on the practice green.

Start the downswing
slowly and smoothly

If you know how you want to play the putt before you swing, you'll find you can execute a smooth, slow-starting downswing with ease. But if you alter your plan in mid-stroke, you'll miss the putt with a jerky downswing. In putting, he who hesitates is lost for sure.

POSITION AT IMPACT

When you meet the ball, your body must be in the same position as it was at the start of the backswing. Many, many putts are missed because the body moves just before the ball is hit. The normal fault is a forward movement, though some players tend to move back from the ball the instant before contact. In either case, the result is almost always a miss.

The only solution is the old reliable: make up your mind in advance that you're not going to move. You won't have time to concentrate on this resolve during the actual swing.

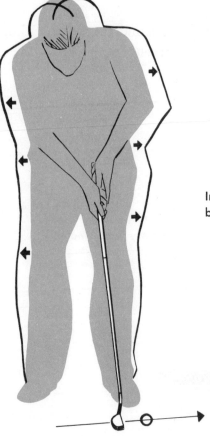

Incorrect: Either a forward sway or a backward movement at impact will nearly always cause a miss

When you miss short putts to the right of the hole, you're probably swaying. This happens when you're overanxious and trying to give the putt a mental "assist."

The best way to avoid this fault is to plant yourself firmly with your weight back over your heels. Move your toes up inside your shoes just after you take your stance. It'll relax you, and you'll know whether your weight's back over your heels.

FOLLOW-THROUGH

The follow-through should be straight along the intended line of flight with the putter face still square to the hole. As with the other strokes the follow-through merely reflects what has gone before. The outcome has already been established.

Imagine the complete putting stroke before you start it.

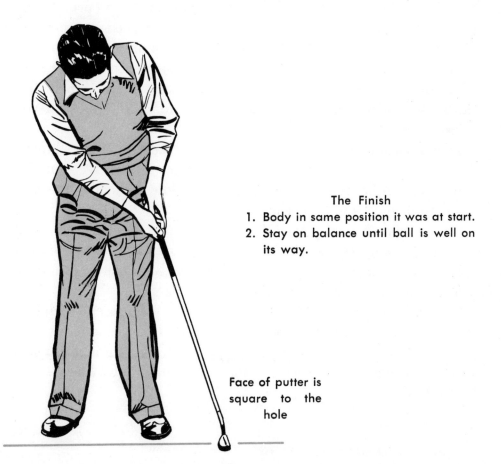

The Finish
1. Body in same position it was at start.
2. Stay on balance until ball is well on its way.

Face of putter is square to the hole

COMPLETION

All that need be said about the completion of the putting stroke is that your body should be in its starting position. Imagine the completion in advance. Like the follow through it merely reflects what has gone before.

Imagine yourself still in balance as the ball is well on its way toward the hole. The completion should reflect a smooth, decisive, confident stroke.

STRATEGY

Effective putting requires more than a sound putting stroke and a sensitive touch—you must also give some thought to the situation at hand. In match play, when you follow an opponent's play and positions as they relate to yours, you can figure out the proper strategy without too much difficulty. For instance, if you need two putts to win the hole from 10 feet out, you know that you must stroke the ball so that it will be as close as possible to the hole for the second putt. Certainly you don't bang the ball for the back of the cup in this situation. Similarly, if you need a 10-footer to tie the hole, all you think about is sinking your one and only.

Even in match play many golfers make mistakes in putting strategy. A player has two putts to win the hole from, say, 20 feet out. He knows that all he has to do is get the ball close enough to the hole for a tap-in and he wins. It looks like a cinch.

To our hypothetical player the approach putt looks so easy that he quits thinking. So he hits the first putt carelessly, leaves himself a 2-footer and then panics when he discovers he might miss and tie a hole that should have been a set-up.

The proper approach in the above situation is to be careful with that first putt. Try to make it so that the ball reaches the hole on its final turn. Remember, if you hand your opponent a hole through careless putting, you not only cost yourself that hole but you give him just the lift he needs.

Tying putts: Many golfers entertain false notions about tying putts in situations where a partner has already tied the hole and you need a putt to win. Don't feel you must get the ball to the hole at any cost. When you hit the ball several feet past the hole, then look up and say, "Well, I gave it a chance," you're only kidding yourself.

Give the ball a chance to get in; let that be your primary objective. Putt boldly, but don't do it just to prove that you're a fearless fellow.

Very long putts: Faced with a long putt from the very edge of the green, many golfers turn to the "hit and hope" method. They make a mountain out of a molehill and give up before they start. Then they simply hit the putt in the general direction of the hole and hope for the best. This is particularly true when a long putt is also very tricky with one or more rolls in the green.

Again, you should settle for nothing less than perfection. Figure the distance and the break(s) as best you can. You'll frequently miscalculate and fail to get the ball close, but then again you'll often

Very long putts—Figure the distance and break as best you can, then hit the ball solidly

figure correctly and lay the ball up dead. Always give the long putt your best try and hit the ball solidly.

Summary: There's no end to the strategic situations that can arise on the green. Some are obvious, others subtle. One cannot hope to cover them all in one book or even a dozen volumes. But the golfer who wants to lower his score and compete successfully against opponents of his own class must always be alert on the greens.

He should understand the tactical situation and know when to exercise caution or boldness without overdoing the one or the other. He should be prepared for abrupt shocks and setbacks such as a successful long putt by an opponent that abruptly changes an easy win into a possible loss. When this happens, he must play as he ordinarily would, making his own best effort.

Q

QUITTING ON THE SHOT: When you quit on a shot, you fail to follow through completely. This fault actually begins before you reach the quitting point. The clubhead falls away about a foot or two past impact and "sticks in the ground." Distance and accuracy are sacrificed.

The best cure is the familiar one of imagining the complete follow through in advance.

Golfers usually "quit" in a tight situation. Maybe you've got to hit the green with an iron shot to match an opponent already up there. Well, you can't "wish" the shot up to the green. So you'd better make up your mind to hit the ball with your best stroke. Even if it goes wrong, at least you will have given it the old college try.

R

RUN-UP SHOT: *See* BANK-CLIMBING SHOT

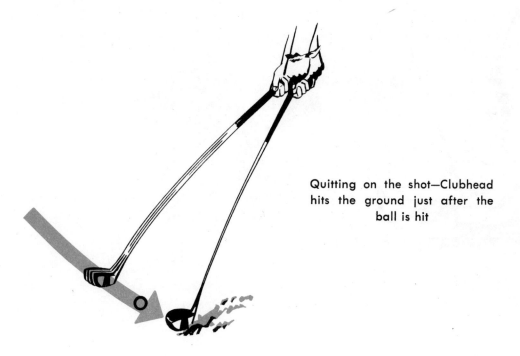

Quitting on the shot—Clubhead
hits the ground just after the
ball is hit

S

SAND TRAPS: The first step in learning to get the ball near the
hole from a sand trap is to develop a shot that will enable you to get
the ball out of the trap and somewhere on the green. After that you
can add refinements that will help you reach a one-putt position.

The texture and depth of the sand affect your distance. Sand that
is wet, coarse, and/or shallow will allow for greater distance than
sand that is deep and powdery, such as newly placed sand. You can
gauge the depth and texture of the sand as you dig in to take your
stance.

The regular explosion is a powerful swing of three-quarter length
so that the clubhead enters the sand behind the ball and never completely contacts the ball itself. You play this shot with the sand wedge.

Sand that is wet, coarse or shallow will allow greater distance

Deep, powdery sand will allow less distance

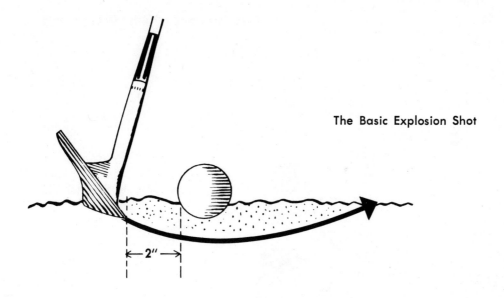

The Basic Explosion Shot

This club has a protruding flange on the bottom that will strike the sand first. With its rounded bottom, the flange will sink only a short way into the sand and help correct an imperfect swing.

The distance you should hit behind the ball will vary from an inch to approximately three and a half inches. The basic distance should be about two inches. Keep your head still and follow through as though you meant it. Take a firm grip. Almost invariably you will hit a lofted shot that will travel between 30 and 100 feet in the air and stop quickly after it lands.

Once you've mastered the basic explosion shot, you can concentrate on getting close to the hole. Experiment with the power of your swing, which ranges from three-quarters for what is termed the regular explosion to less than half for the soft explosion. Use the full power swing to get out of a particularly tough spot or to obtain maximum distance. Experiment with the two-inch margin between the ball and the point where the clubhead strikes the sand. Touch is very important here.

In making an explosion shot, remember:

(*1*) Your stance should be slightly open (left foot withdrawn from the line), your feet about shoulder width between the insteps.

(*2*) Your feet should be planted firmly enough in the sand to provide firm footing throughout the swing.

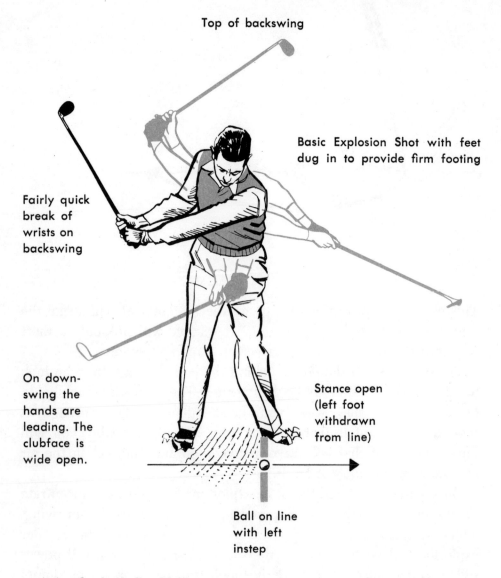

Top of backswing

Basic Explosion Shot with feet
dug in to provide firm footing

Fairly quick
break of
wrists on
backswing

On down-
swing the
hands are
leading. The
clubface is
wide open.

Stance open
(left foot
withdrawn
from line)

Ball on line
with left
instep

(3) The ball should be approximately on line with your left instep for level lie.

(4) Break your wrists and hands quickly on the backswing.

(5) On the downswing your hands should be out in front of the left arm, as when you are trying to obtain added loft on a pitch shot.

(6) Keep a consistently firm grip throughout your stroke.

(7) To be on the safe side, start your swing with the clubface slightly open and finish it with the palm of your left hand down so that the clubface remains open during the entire swing.

Basic Explosion Shot showing ball rising from trap on top of the sand

Golfers who fear sand traps or find themselves in the throes of a sand slump should go in for practice sessions of thirty minutes or so. Practice swinging without a ball until you are able to take sand divots of uniform size—an inch to three-quarters of an inch deep and six inches long—in a straight line. Use a full follow-through each time. Then try it with a ball.

TYPICAL SAND TRAP PROBLEMS

Following are some typical sand trap problems that you're likely to encounter in one form or another:

Situation: Normal lie in dry sand of average texture.*

Solution: This is the basic sand trap shot, the one most golfers encounter most often. So it calls for the regular explosion shot.

Pick out a spot about two inches behind the ball. With your eyes glued to the spot *and* the ball, use three-quarter power to bring the clubhead in contact with the sand at the vital spot. With head stationary, swing under and through the ball. Take out a divot of sand about six inches long and in a straight line with your objective

---

* A normal lie in dry sand means that one-eighth of the ball is hidden by sand.

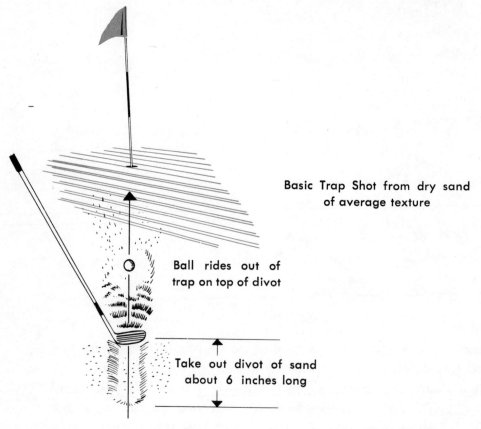

Basic Trap Shot from dry sand of average texture

Ball rides out of trap on top of divot

Take out divot of sand about 6 inches long

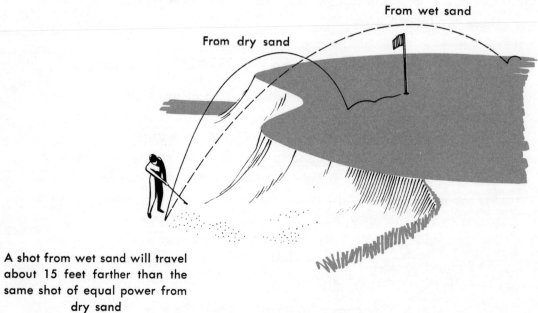

From wet sand

From dry sand

A shot from wet sand will travel about 15 feet farther than the same shot of equal power from dry sand

(if the sand is normally dry, the sand divot will fall apart before you see it, but envision taking the divot anyway). Picture the ball as it rides out of the sand trap on top of the divot. You can only judge distance from sand traps through touch and consequently practice.

Situation: Normal lie in wet sand that's not soggy.

Solution: Use a regular explosion with some slight adjustment. Wet sand is more tightly packed than dry sand. Hence the clubhead of your sand wedge will not dig as deeply into the sand before moving forward. The clubhead should enter the sand about one-fourth of an inch farther back from the ball than it would in normal dry sand (the divot on which the ball rises will be thinner and firmer, giving it greater propulsion and distance).

You need a strong follow-through with a steady grip to take the clubhead through the wet sand. A wet sand shot will generally travel some fifteen feet farther than a dry sand shot. Moreover, it will have a lot of underspin, causing the ball to stop quickly after it lands.

Situation: A normal lie in a trap where the sand is shallow (two inches deep or less).

Solution: A soft explosion shot is what you want here. Dig the clubhead into the sand at the normal two-inch distance behind the ball. But swing more easily than you would in sand of normal depth—the flange of your wedge will probably strike firm ground soon after

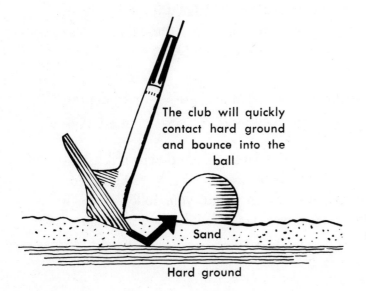

The club will quickly contact hard ground and bounce into the ball

Sand

Hard ground

In traps where sand is shallow, swing easier—This is the "Soft" Explosion Shot contact and bounce forward into the ball. This shot can be treacherous, and the easy swing is your safeguard.

Follow through in the normal manner. Nearly all the traps on some courses are shallow, and on many courses with traps of normal sand depth the edges of the traps are shallow. Test the depth of the sand as you dig in with your feet.

Situation: The ball is buried deep in sand so that the top of the ball is even with the top of the sand.

Solution: Use a strong explosion. Close the clubface slightly to produce a more pronounced digging angle. Use a full power swing. Fix your eyes on the spot where the clubhead will enter the sand— as close to the ball as possible as long as you don't hit the ball first. Try to send the clubhead under and past the ball, keeping your eyes fixed on the spot where it enters the sand.

You must keep your head still. Remember, the ball will have little underspin so it will roll some after it hits.

Situation: The ball is deeply buried in heavy sand so that the top of the ball is visible but below the top level of sand.

Solution: Use a strong explosion with pitching wedge or 9-iron. The sharper leading edge of these clubs will enable you to penetrate deeper into the sand. Your problem is simple: to escape from the trap and the position you are in.

Don't panic and take a wild swing just because your situation seems impossible. You'll need smooth power to dislodge the ball. Dig as deeply behind the ball as you can and still follow through. Be very careful not to hit the ball before you hit the sand. Otherwise you may drive it in deeper.

Situation: The ball is about half buried, and there's a slight depression around it—say six inches across—caused by the ball's impact (this is called the "fried egg" lie).

Solution: A strong explosion is the answer. Use a downward, chopping stroke. Position the ball at the center of the feet. Since you must dig the clubhead well down into the sand, your follow-through will be somewhat restricted. However, you should follow through as much as possible.

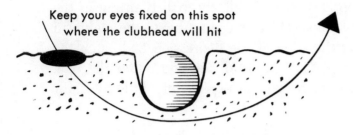

Keep your eyes fixed on this spot where the clubhead will hit

Close the clubface slightly, use a full-power swing to dig the ball out of a deeply buried lie

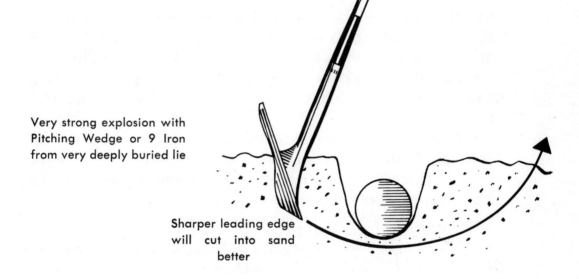

Very strong explosion with Pitching Wedge or 9 Iron from very deeply buried lie

Sharper leading edge will cut into sand better

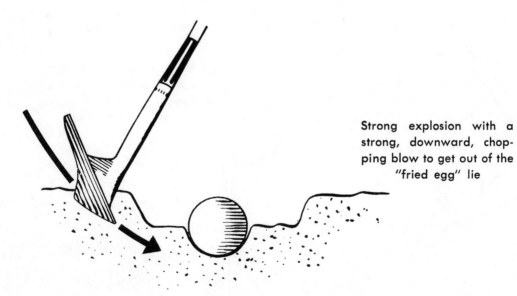

Strong explosion with a strong, downward, chopping blow to get out of the "fried egg" lie

You won't get much underspin on this shot, so allow for some roll.

Why a downward, chopping blow? Well, the ball is sitting in the center of a two-level depression. On a sweeping blow, the clubhead would contact the sand at the edge of the depression and catch the ball in the center or on top. The clubhead must go under the ball. Be cautious on this shot, though you can expect very little accuracy in placing it.

Situation: The ball is exposed on a downslope (downhill lie).

Solution: Use a regular explosion shot with adjustments. When you play from a downhill lie in the sand, the depth of the sand decreases from the point where the clubhead penetrates. Therefore, the clubhead should enter the sand farther behind the ball than it would on a level lie shot. Approximately a half inch farther back is about right.

Put a little extra weight on your right foot to keep from swaying forward, which you'll tend to do if your left foot is on a lower level than the right.

Remember that a shot from a downhill lie will normally produce little loft. If you need much loft, open the clubface a few extra degrees. This will tend to direct the ball more to the right, so take it into account when lining up for the shot.

Situation: The ball is exposed on an upslope (uphill lie).

Solution: Again, use the regular explosion with adjustments. On an uphill lie shot, make the clubhead enter the sand a little closer

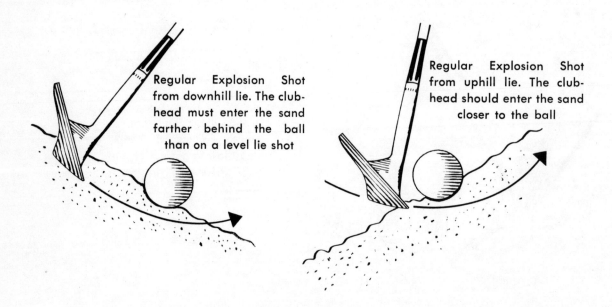

Regular Explosion Shot from downhill lie. The clubhead must enter the sand farther behind the ball than on a level lie shot

Regular Explosion Shot from uphill lie. The clubhead should enter the sand closer to the ball to the ball because the sand is deeper from the point of entry. Approximately a half inch closer is about right.

You must also adjust your stance. Standing on an upslope, you will be canted backward. Place most of your weight forward on the left foot.

Remember that the deeper sand will slow up the clubhead, so you've got to put a little extra effort into your follow-through.

Situation: The ball is completely exposed on flat sand. There's no high obstacle along the intended line of flight, and there's room on the green for a lot of roll.

Solution: Under these conditions you can use a chip shot from sand. For this shot, your weight is mostly on the left foot. Position the ball in the center of the feet at address. Remember that you *must* hit the ball before you strike sand; otherwise the sand will stymie your clubhead.

This is a delicate operation, so if you have any questions about it use the safer explosion shot.

Keep your eyes glued to the top of the ball

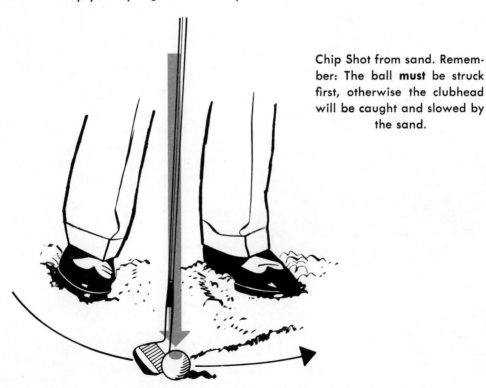

Chip Shot from sand. Remember: The ball **must** be struck first, otherwise the clubhead will be caught and slowed by the sand.

Fix your eyes on top of the ball rather than behind it to insure immediate contact.

You can use any one of your more lofted clubs (from the 7-iron through the wedges) on the chip. It depends on how much roll you want. Grip the club farther down on the shaft than you would for an ordinary chip from grass. Otherwise the shot is virtually the same —a crisp downward blow.

Situation: The ball is fully exposed on flat or nearly flat sand. A smooth, gradual upslope leads out of the trap, and there's no overhanging lip.

Solution: You can use a putter in this situation. Be careful to hit the ball solidly in the center. If you hit it above center, you'll drive it into the sand. If you hit it too much below center, you'll loft it a few feet and it'll stick in the sand again. Aim to keep the ball rolling along on top of the sand.

This is a dangerous shot in soft sand. It works best in damp, hard or shallow sand. When well executed, this shot will work on any

Putt out of a trap, if there is no overhanging lip, the sand is flat, and the side of the green smooth.

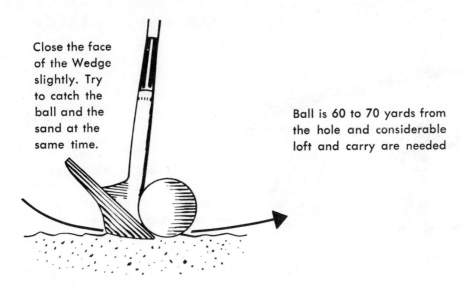

Close the face of the Wedge slightly. Try to catch the ball and the sand at the same time.

Ball is 60 to 70 yards from the hole and considerable loft and carry are needed

bank of less than 90 degrees incline, but the trap must be relatively shallow and next to the green.

If you use your putter wisely, you can succeed on this shot. But the conditions must be just right.

Situation: The ball is about 60 to 75 yards from the hole. The shot requires considerable loft and carry, though it's hardly a full one.

Solution: This is one of the hardest shots in golf. Close the face of the wedge slightly and try to catch the ball and the sand at the same time. Gauge your distance as you would for a shot from the rough of the same length.

When the lie is clean, you can hit the ball first and judge the distance fairly accurately. If the lie is slightly buried, try to meet the ball immediately following contact with the sand. Your power should be in proportion to the amount of sand you must penetrate. Plan the shot with care, and then swing with confident deliberation.

Situation: You have a good clean lie calling for maximum long-iron or medium-iron distance, and there's no high bank in front of you.

Solution: Dig in well with your feet or they'll shift when you rotate. The shot is similar to the same shot from the fairway, but try to swing with your arms and shoulders to prevent slipping in loose sand. Your best bet is to try to pick off the ball cleanly, taking only a divot of sand in front of the ball.

Good, clean lie with long iron or medium iron. Distance needed. Try to make swing largely with the arms and shoulders. Pick the ball off sand cleanly.

Swing well within your maximum power, taking plenty of club. (The same stroke pattern applies to short iron (6-7-8-9) shots from sand, though you can play these with a fairly high bank in front of you.)

Situation: The ball is completely exposed and exceptionally well positioned. There are no obstacles ahead, and you need maximum distance.

Solution: Use a 3 or 4-wood. Get as firm a footing as possible. Open the clubface slightly to allow for a small slice or fade. The clubhead will contact the sand sole first so that it will bounce or slide into the ball even if you hit slightly behind it.

Swing well within your maximum power, and keep your eyes glued on the back of the ball.

Don't try this shot unless conditions are ideal. If you have any doubts, use one of your deeper irons.

Situation: The ball is perched atop a windblown ridge on the edge of a footprint or some similar depression left in the trap.

Solution: Use a soft explosion. With very little sand under the ball, you must ease up the stroke. If you play the shot right, the clubhead will almost certainly meet the ball; if the clubhead enters the sand a normal distance behind the ball, it may slide all the way under and send the ball only two or three feet. Swing slightly harder than you

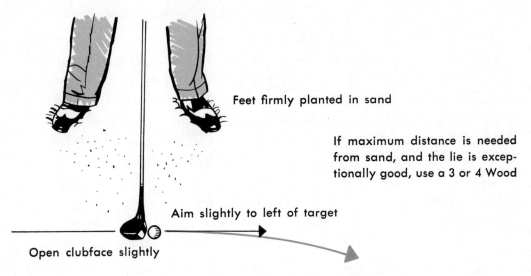

Feet firmly planted in sand

If maximum distance is needed from sand, and the lie is exceptionally good, use a 3 or 4 Wood

Aim slightly to left of target

Open clubface slightly

Ball will fade or slice a little

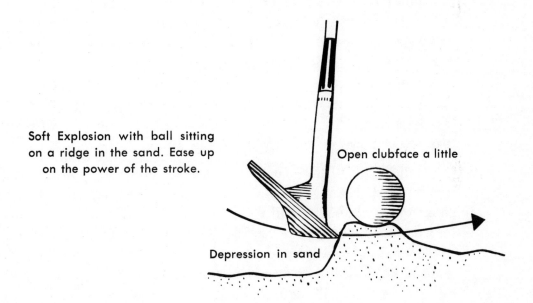

Soft Explosion with ball sitting on a ridge in the sand. Ease up on the power of the stroke.

Open clubface a little

Depression in sand

would for a similar grass shot. Open the clubface a few extra degrees to add loft and cut down on distance.

Sometimes you should use a pitching wedge or 9-iron on this shot because of the lighter head. You may find it almost impossible to swing the heavier headed sand wedge easily enough to produce the desired distance (flange or lack of it aside).

Situation: The ball is in a foot or heel print.

Solution: Use a regular or strong explosion. Treat this shot the same as you would the buried lie, except that you may exaggerate the downward, chopping stroke if the clubhead must enter the sand within the boundaries of the depression. If the ball is at the edge of the depression, play the shot the same as you would a buried lie. The idea is to get the clubhead under the ball without touching it.

A cut-across action may prove helpful here if you want to avoid striking high sand at the edge of the depression. In that case, open the stance more by drawing the left foot farther back from the line so that your hands will have more leeway coming across the line.

Situation: The ball is very close to the edge of the green, and the pin is spotted near the trap.

Solution: Use a soft explosion with a deliberately shortened follow-through (the clubhead should go only about three feet past the ball). Otherwise this shot is the same one you'd use for a normal sand shot where greater distance is required. Use this method only when the carry you need to reach the green is no more than 8 feet and the flag is 20 feet or less from the edge of the trap near you.

This is a special kind of sand shot. You'll seldom need to use it. It's easier and safer to restrict the follow-through on this little shot than to cut down on the power of your swing.

Situation: You're faced with a normal lie in a very powdery trap.

Solution: Use a regular explosion, remembering that the clubhead enters the sand about a half inch closer to the ball than is customary for a normal dry sand shot. The clubhead will sink in deeper, so you'll have more sand to dig out along with the ball. The divot will disintegrate rapidly, adding little momentum to the ball. A normal lie in this type of sand will hide anywhere from one-sixth to one-fourth of the ball.

The sand will be soft and powdery when it's first placed in the trap. Moreover, certain sections of the country use this type of small-grained sand. Your feet will sink in quickly, but dig in even more for a firm footing.

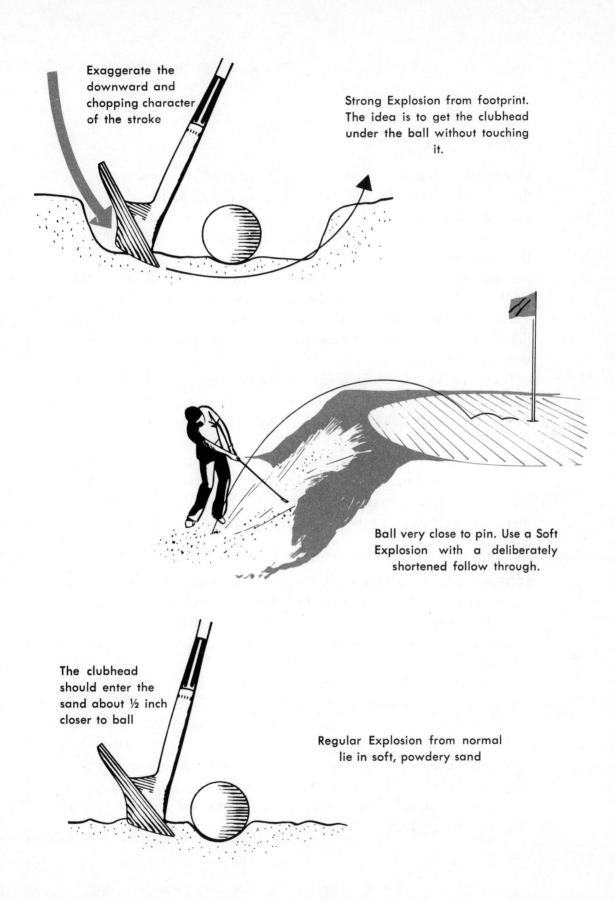

Exaggerate the downward and chopping character of the stroke

Strong Explosion from footprint. The idea is to get the clubhead under the ball without touching it.

Ball very close to pin. Use a Soft Explosion with a deliberately shortened follow through.

The clubhead should enter the sand about ½ inch closer to ball

Regular Explosion from normal lie in soft, powdery sand

SAND WEDGE: *See* CLUBS

SCLAFFING: Sclaffing is an early golf term which denotes hitting the ground behind the ball. This fault is related to the skied shot (*see* SKYING THE BALL).

Unless the error is great, this fault will sometimes right itself with the wood clubs. The clubhead may strike the ground with the smooth sole making the first contact, then bounce on into the ball for a fairly good shot. But with the irons, the error is usually fatal.

The causes here are basically the same as for the skied shot except that the error is more pronounced. You want to add power so inevitably you drop that right shoulder, and that does it.

The remedies for sclaffing and skying are pretty much the same. Swing with controlled power. Depend on the real sources of your power that are explained in SWING (GENERAL). Keep your head stationary, and hit through the ball.

The fault can crop up again when you tee the ball the wrong way. If the ball is teed too low for the drive, there's precious little margin for error on impact, and the clubhead will hit the ground before it meets the ball. Medium height teeing is best for the drive.

SCORING RANGE: This section covers the little shots that help lower your score—the approach shots, chips and pitches that constitute your short game. I'm excluding sand shots and putts, which are discussed in SAND TRAPS and PUTTING, so that we can concentrate specifically on the short swing.

Any duffer can develop an effective short game around the greens. The longer shots require a coordination of muscle and eye (and to some extent strength) that some golfers do not have. But the swing for shots around the green doesn't require a lot of strength or muscular coordination. Even the poorest golfer has an opportunity to improve his score and offset the effects of an otherwise disappointing game. So if you're just hobbling along on your drives, the shorter strokes can be your big game.

Right shoulder dropped far too much

Hitting behind the ball

Ball is here ———————————

Clubhead hits here — — — — —

Ball teed too low

The proper grip for short shots is the same as outlined in the section on GRIP. The only difference is that you grip the club about three inches lower on the shaft. The hands should be slightly forward of the clubhead.

The stance should be open with the left foot withdrawn some six inches from the line. This open stance enables you to partially face the hole so that you can keep the ball on the proper line. Your heels should be about three inches apart, your toes turned out. Stand sufficiently erect to allow for a full extension of the arms. The weight should remain on the heels.

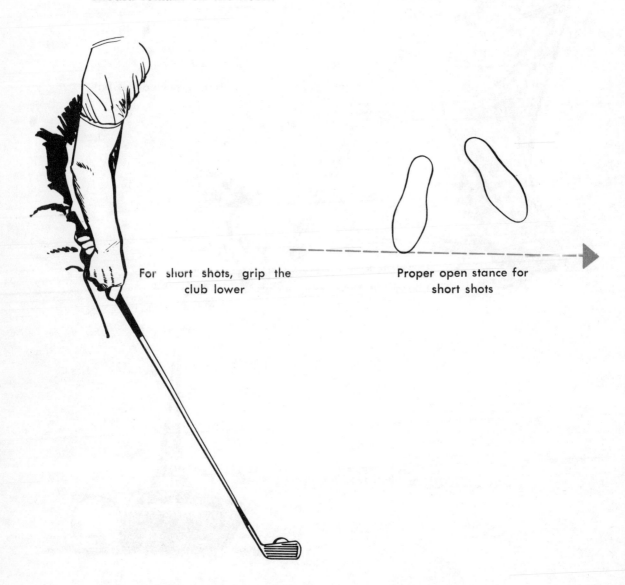

For short shots, grip the club lower

Proper open stance for short shots

For the basic stroke, swing the
club back on a line straight back
from the ball

Head must be
firmly anchored

The stroke should be firm and
crisp, but smooth and unhurried

Swing the club back in line with the ball. The downswing and
follow-through should be straight toward the target. The over-all
stroke is firm and crisp, though smooth and unhurried. Make the
swing all of a piece—no sudden added power, no letting up.

Keep your head still. Then you'll hit the ball solidly each time with
plenty of "touch."

You execute your short shots around the green with your arms
and hands. Body rotation is kept to the minimum. Any lateral movement of the body is likely to be disastrous, for then you hit either too
far behind the ball (the poop shot) or too high up on the ball (blading
the shot). Pooping results from too much backward lateral shift. An
excessive forward lateral shift causes blading. (Because there's no
need to shift your weight in the first place, there's no sense in talking
about compensating for the shift.) Remember, when you do turn
your body, it's harder to keep the ball in line with the target.

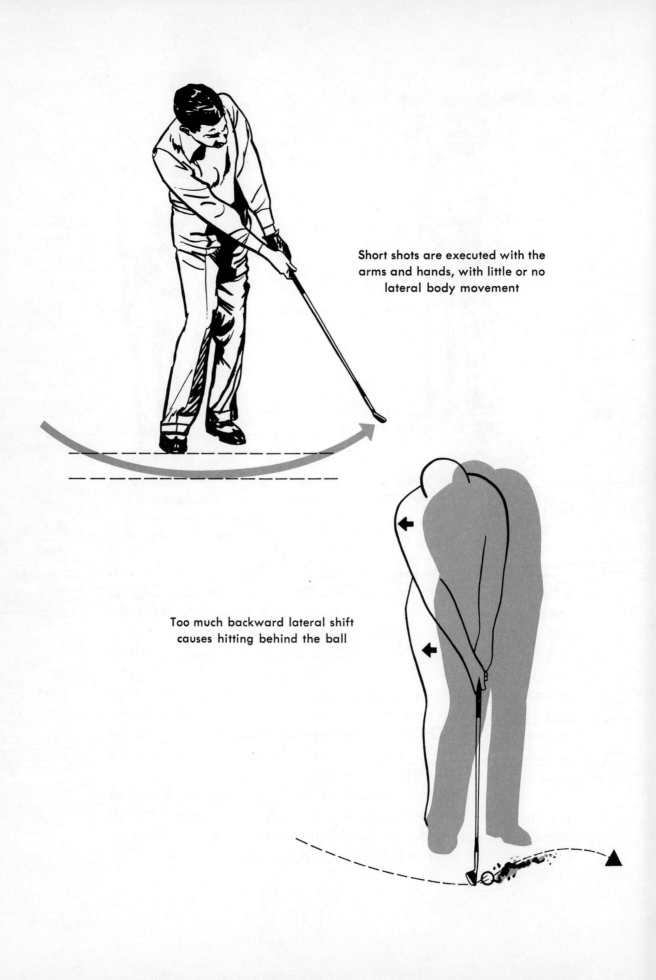

Short shots are executed with the
arms and hands, with little or no
lateral body movement

Too much backward lateral shift
causes hitting behind the ball

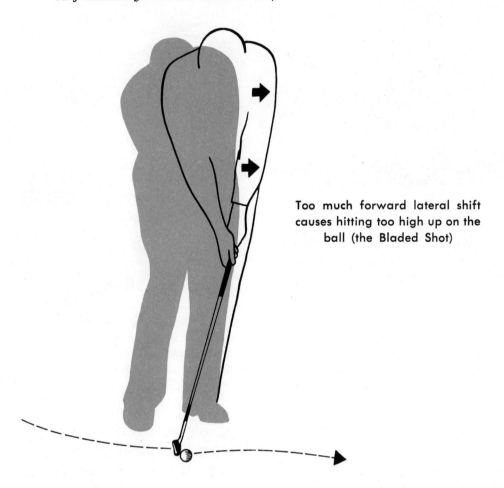

Too much forward lateral shift causes hitting too high up on the ball (the Bladed Shot)

Planning is the key to effective play in the scoring range. You must plan the shot in detail. How far should the ball travel in the air and how far should it roll? Once you've made up your mind, stick to it. If you suddenly change your plan while making the shot, you won't put the ball where you want to.

Sometimes when a player reaches the top of his backswing, he worries about leaving the ball short of the hole. Tightening his grip, he jerkily speeds up his downswing, and the ball scuds well past the hole, possibly on over the green.

On the other hand, he may feel that his backswing is too long and he's going to knock the ball too far. So he makes the fatal error of letting up, and the ball "poops out" before it can cover the required distance.

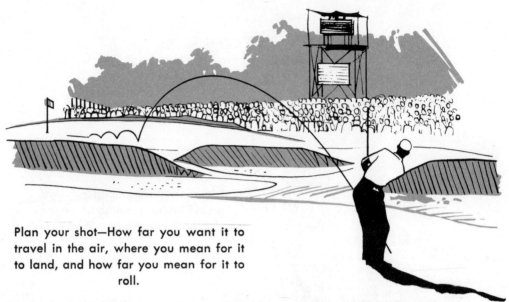

Plan your shot—How far you want it to travel in the air, where you mean for it to land, and how far you mean for it to roll.

On the final hole at Inverness in the 1957 Open, I used a Pitching Wedge from 40 yards out to get over a large trap and bunker in front of the green. My ball hit about 15 feet to the right of the pin, and I had planned that the slant of the green would bring it down into the cup. It did a little, but not as much as I was counting on, and I was left with about a nine foot putt.

You've got to select the right club, keeping in mind (*1*) how far inside the front of the green the ball should first land, (*2*) how much underspin the club will normally put on the ball and (*3*) what the normal loft will be. You should be able to judge the roll to expect for, say, a 5-iron, if you want to reach a certain spot on the green. All this is a matter of touch.

Many players have a favorite club for the simple shots around the green. However, you should let the conditions of the shot dictate the choice of your club.

THREE-QUARTER AND HALF SHOTS

The three-quarter shot and half shot are also included in the scoring range. For golfers who shoot for a normal distance, the range is between 40-90 yards. I realize that some golfers, particularly among the ladies, must hit full shots from 90 yards and under. But I'm speaking here of the range that doesn't require a full swing to reach the hole.

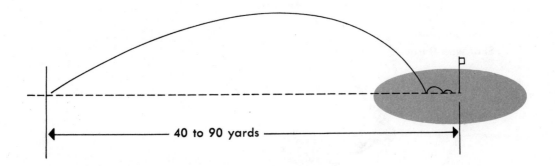

Yardage for Half and Three-quarter Shots. These shots are at the outer edge of the scoring range.

I will take up the three-quarter and half shot together because they are virtually identical in technique. Moreover, they overlay in the sense that a half shot for one player may be a three-quarter shot for another, etc. The average golfer encounters a great many of these shots on his third shot on a par-five hole—providing he has hit a reasonably long drive and second. The shot offers the average player some of his best birdie chances.

Actually, the terms three-quarter and half apply mostly to the length of the swing rather than the power behind it. In other words, you cut down the length of the backswing by one-quarter or one-half to play the shot as it should be played. You should guard against taking the normal length backswing and then trying to reduce distance by letting up on the force of the swing. True, you don't swing as hard on this kind of shot as on the regular full shot. But, as stated above, the differences are in the length of the swing.

On full shots you hit the ball with your full power. But in the medium range you must decide *how much* power you must apply. This necessarily complicates your decision.

What you must do is imagine the amount of power you think you need to apply to the stroke. You must do this before you begin the actual stroke. And for heaven's sake, don't change your mind in mid-swing so that you lunge or let up.

The swing for the three-quarter and half shots is the same as for full shots. So are the stance, grip and other fundamentals.

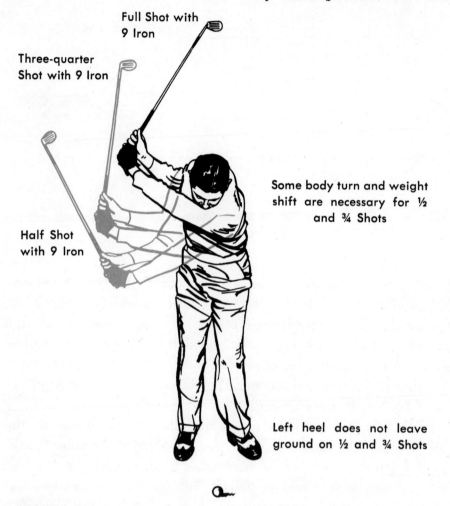

The three-quarter and half shots require some body rotation and weight transference. The three-quarter shot calls for the three-quarter body turn and weight shift used in the full shot. However, you don't have to raise the left heel off the ground to make the turn.

PITCH AND CHIP SHOTS

Most players think of the pitch as a well lofted shot that stops rather quickly after it lands. The chip is generally regarded as a low trajectory shot that rolls a good bit after it hits. Some call any high shot with one of the shorter irons a "pitch shot." When I use the term "pitch" in this section, I'm referring to a high, short shot around the green. There

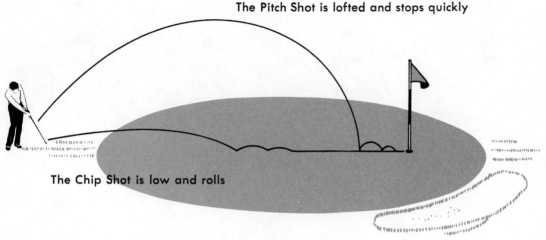

The Pitch Shot is lofted and stops quickly

The Chip Shot is low and rolls

Difference between a Pitch and a Chip

is no need to differentiate strongly between the pitch and chip. They are played with the same basic stroke.

SCORING RANGE SITUATIONS

We are agreed, I trust, that these shots from up close can lower your golf score. There are, of course, an infinite variety of problems to be encountered around the green—simple shots, tough shots, in-between shots, shots that should roll most of the way to the hole, shots that should stop quickly after the ball lands, etc.

The examples that follow cover the *basic* situations you will meet. If you study them, you can improve your short game.

Situation: The ball is 10 feet short of a level, non-elevated, medium-speed green. The flag is 40 feet back on the green. The lie is good. There's no bunker or other obstacle between the ball and the edge of the green.

Solution: These are the conditions of a *basic, simple chip*. Plan the shot. Remember that it is simple and you don't want to complicate it. Pick out a spot 8 to 15 feet past the edge of the green. Then pick a club that will give the ball just enough roll from that spot to send it to the hole. Remember your trajectory and the speed of the green.

Strike the ball with a crisp downward blow, following through in line with the hole.

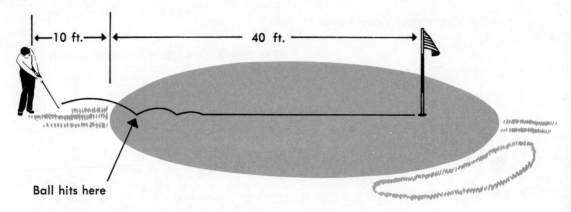

Simple, basic Chip Shot

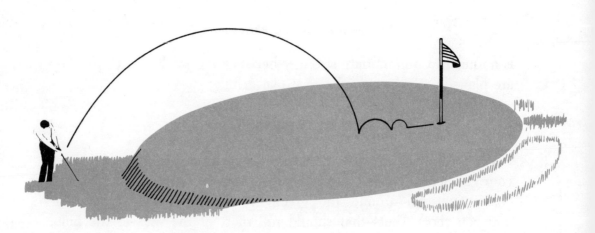

Shot out of high grass with deeply lofted club

Situation: The ball is in the normal chipping position but in deep grass; there are no intervening obstacles.

Solution: This is a regular chip shot with adjustments. A deeply lofted club will quickly lift the ball up and out of grass. This is essentially a right-hand shot. So grip the club with a slight extra pressure in the fingers of the right hand. The stroke should be crisp and firm. If there is any looseness as you come into the ball through the deep grass, you may be turning the clubhead too much or slowing it down, possibly both. Take a reasonably short backswing, strike a crisp downward blow and complete the swing with a follow-through toward the hole. If you're afraid of knocking the ball too far, keep the clubface slightly open throughout the swing by not letting your hands roll over.

Situation: The ball is in deep grass behind a bunker.

Solution: Select your deepest club, open the clubface slightly for immediate height and position the ball near your left toe to insure contact at the very end of the downstroke. Exert slight extra pressure in fingers of your right hand, as you would for a similar shot with no intervening bunker.

Situation: The ball is about 50 feet short of the green; the flag is some 15 feet from the front edge. A level fairway intervenes.

Solution: Use the chip and run. Under normal conditions, it would be hard to pitch the ball onto the green from this position and have it stop quickly enough. In general, it's wiser to let the ball hit in front of the green and roll on. *Determine your trajectory and landing spot,*

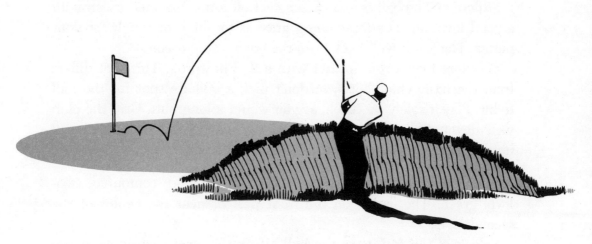

Use deepest club to pitch out of high grass from behind bunker

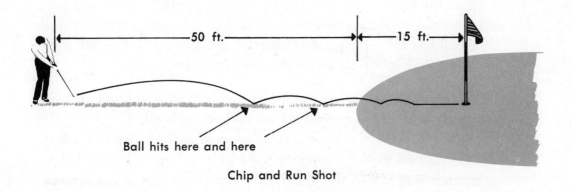

Ball hits here and here

Chip and Run Shot

and then stick to your decision. This shot is difficult because it is all but impossible to judge exactly how the ball will bounce when it hits even the smoothest of fairways. The ball's underspin makes it difficult to judge the bounce. So keep your underspin *down.*

Don't try to eliminate underspin altogether with a straight-faced club. The more the ball bounces—and it must bounce several times if it travels most of the distance along the ground—the more chances you take. Try to hit a happy medium between pitch and run. Choose a club that won't give you too much underspin but will send the ball through the air for most of the distance. The distance of your pitch shot is a matter of individual judgment. Pick a spot where the ground is uniform and likely to provide the expected bounce.

Situation: The ball is one to four feet off a non-elevated green with a good level lie. The intervening grass is too high or rough for your putter. The pin is well back from the edge of the green.

Solution: Play a run-up shot with a 2, 3 or 4-iron. This shot differs from the basic chip shot—you don't pick a definite spot for the ball to hit. Play it solely by touch, as you would a long putt. Grip the club well down. Follow through toward the hole. Keep your head still until after you've hit the ball.

Situation: The ball is just short of a non-elevated, contoured, two-level green. The flag is on the front part or near the center of the second level.

Solution: You can make the ball hit on the level part of the green and run up the slope to the hole. Or you can pitch over the slope with a more lofted club that gives a pronounced underspin. A run-up shot in which the ball hits short of the upslope is generally safest and best under normal conditions. Choose a club that will permit sufficient roll if the ball hits three or four feet short of the upslope. If the ball *does* hit the upslope, it will travel roughly the same distance.

Situation: The ball is just short of a non-elevated, contoured, two-level green with the flag well back on the second level.

Solution: A pitch over the intervening upslope would be most effective. It's difficult to judge distance for a long roll up a slope followed by another long roll to the pin. This is especially true if the upslope

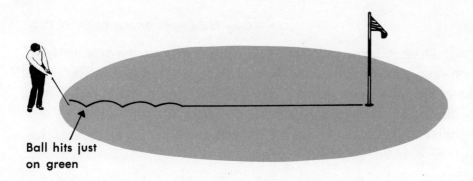

**Ball hits just
on green**

Run-up Shot from good lie with low iron

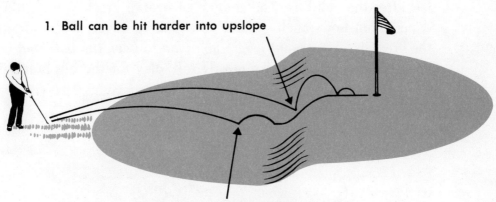

1. Ball can be hit harder into upslope

2. Or ball can hit short of upslope and roll up to hole

Run-up Shot on two-level green can be
hit two ways with same club

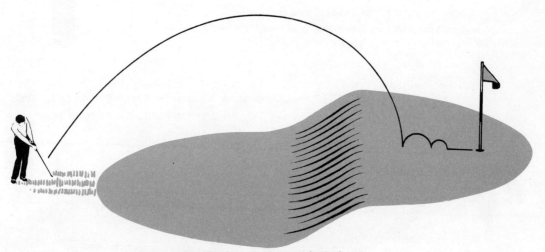

Pitch with Wedge onto second level
when the pin is well back

is fairly steep. Choose a lofted club—a pitching wedge is your best choice—and pick out a spot safely past the upslope. Stick to the principles of the simple chip stroke.

Note: If the flag is near the back of the green, it may be wise to use the pitch and run shot that hits short of the slope. This eliminates the danger of pitching behind the green.

Situation: The ball is just short of a green that slants to the right or left from your position.

Solution: Use a regular chip shot, allowing for a roll to the right or left after the ball hits. The amount of overall break you should play depends on how much ground you plan to cover in the air. Judge the break *from the point where you plan to have the ball land* on the green. If your shot is to be mostly roll, play for the big break; if it's

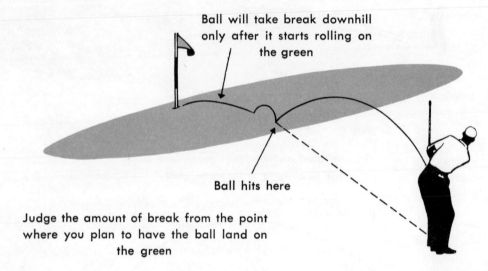

Ball will take break downhill only after it starts rolling on the green

Ball hits here

Judge the amount of break from the point where you plan to have the ball land on the green

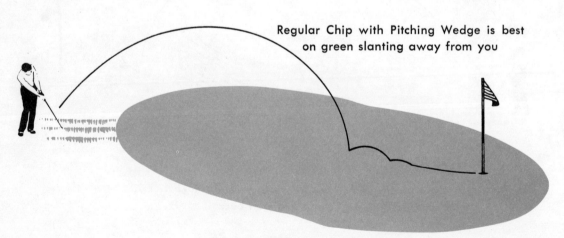

Regular Chip with Pitching Wedge is best on green slanting away from you

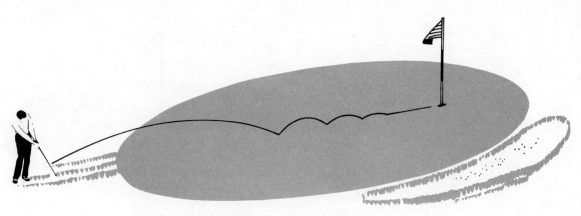

Regular Chip on green that slants uphill. Be careful not to choose too lofted a club, one that will give you too much backspin, causing you to stop short

mostly pitch, play for a small break. Remember, as long as the ball is travelling fairly fast, it will resist breaking. Only after it settles down to a fairly slow roll along the ground (instead of bouncing) will it take the full break.

Situation: The ball is just short of a green that slants away (downhill) from your position.

Solution: Use the regular chip shot, but always use one of your more lofted clubs. The ball will lose its underspin when it hits on a downslope. Finish with the palm of your left hand down so that you don't close the clubface by turning your hands over as you meet the shot. The pitching wedge is your best club for chips onto greens that slant away from you.

Situation: The ball is just short of a green that slants uphill from your position.

Solution: Use a regular chip shot, but be careful not to choose too lofted a club so that you get more underspin on the ball than you need. The underspin will work well for you when the ball hits an upslope. If the flag is well back from your position, toe in the clubhead slightly and let your hands roll over slightly as you go through the ball. This will insure a good roll.

Situation: The ball is in a basic chipping position but lies uphill.

Solution: Use a regular chip shot with one of your less lofted clubs. The angle of incline will increase the height of your shot and the

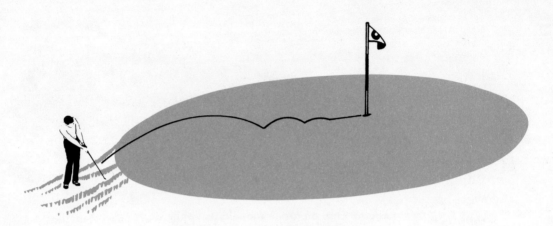

Regular Chip with a less lofted club from an uphill lie

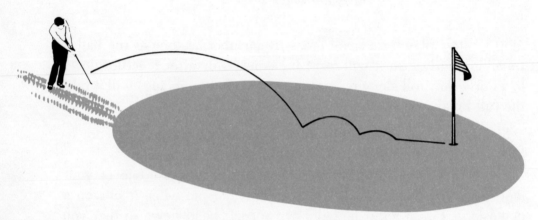

Normal Chip with deeply lofted club from downhill lie

amount of underspin on the ball. The pitching wedge or 9-iron is seldom your most effective weapon in this situation unless you only need ten feet of roll and under.

Situation: The ball is on a downhill lie within chipping distance. There are no intervening bunkers or other obstacles.

Solution: Use a normal chip with a deep, lofted club. Unless you make a special effort to lift the ball, it will come off the downhill lie in a low trajectory and then roll. Choose a club two or three numbers higher than the one you'd use for the same shot off a level lie. If the downhill lie is pronounced, move the ball back toward your right heel so you'll catch it at the end of the shortened downstroke. You should play the average downhill lie from the normal chipping stance.

Situation: The ball is on a pronounced downhill lie and you need loft.

Solution: Open the face of your pitching wedge to the widest angle and use a cut-across stroke. Your stance is quite open. Take back the clubhead well outside the line. The downswing is from the outside in. Your wide open stance enables you to continue your follow through across the ball. Adjust your aim by standing as though you were about to shoot to the left of the target to compensate for the open clubface. This will send the ball to the right. Try to meet the ball at the lowest possible point. If the shot is played properly, the ball is likely to bounce to the right because of the spin. When you take aim, make allowances for this. The angle of incline tells you how much to open the clubface. If the lie is fairly close, you can hardly open the clubface too much. But if the ball sits well up in deep grass, the clubhead could slide under it and make little or no contact.

Situation: The short approach shot with the ball well above the feet.

Solution: You must allow for a natural tendency to pull the ball to the left. The flat swing you need for contact may pull on you. If

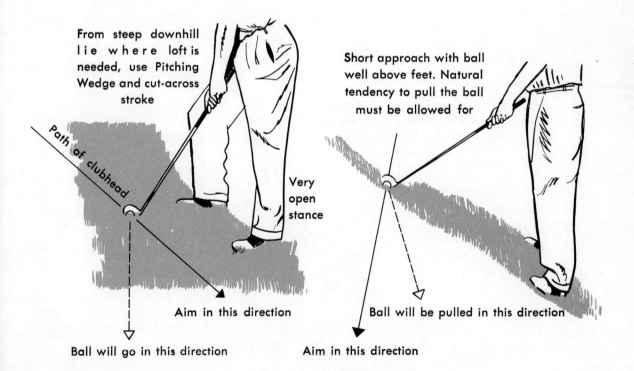

From steep downhill lie where loft is needed, use Pitching Wedge and cut-across stroke

Path of clubhead

Very open stance

Aim in this direction

Ball will go in this direction

Short approach with ball well above feet. Natural tendency to pull the ball must be allowed for

Ball will be pulled in this direction

Aim in this direction

you've got to make a 60-foot shot at knee level, the pull will be from three to five feet. You can compensate for this by (1) opening the clubface about 10 degrees and keeping it open throughout your swing or (2) allow for aiming a few feet to the right with a normal swing.

Situation: The short approach shot with the ball well below the feet.

Solution: Don't let your weight move forward during the swing so that the clubhead meets the ball too near the shaft—you'll shank. You can guard against this by moving in close to the ball and keeping your weight back on your heels throughout the swing. Since your swing is more upright, you may push the ball slightly to the right. Aim two or three feet to the left of the hole.

Situation: The ball is at the base of a steep bank of green or directly behind a high bunker, necessitating a quick and pronounced loft.

Solution: Select your deepest club and add to your loft by opening the clubface 15 to 20 degrees. Open your stance and position the ball even with or slightly ahead of the left toe. The clubhead shouldn't contact the ball until it is about halfway under it. Keep your clubface open during the shot. If the bank or bunker retards your follow-

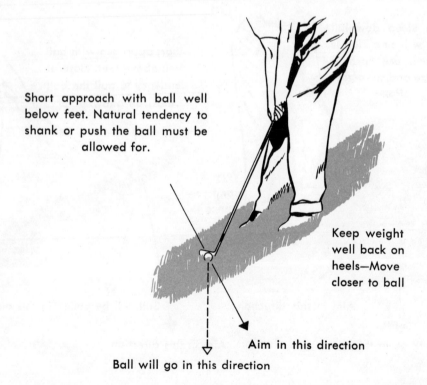

Short approach with ball well below feet. Natural tendency to shank or push the ball must be allowed for.

Keep weight well back on heels—Move closer to ball

Aim in this direction

Ball will go in this direction

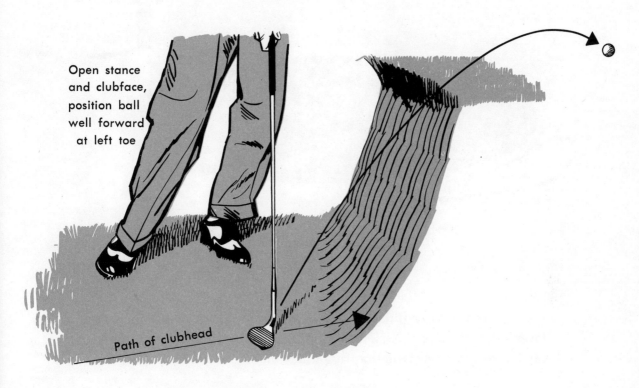

Open stance and clubface, position ball well forward at left toe

Path of clubhead

Chip from behind steep bank, where quick loft is needed

through, hit on into the bank or bunker without slowing up. Trust the loft of your club to raise the ball—don't try to lift it out with your hands.

Situation: The ball is no more than seven or eight feet off the green. The grass between your position and the green proper is cut fairly close and the ground is even and fairly level.

Solution: Use your putter as an approach club, handling it as you would any long approach putt. Keep your eyes on the back of the ball so you can hit it solidly.

The ground you have to cover has two rolling speeds. It's slower up to the edge of the green.

Trust in your sense of touch, and try for perfection. Think of the last turn into the front of the cup.

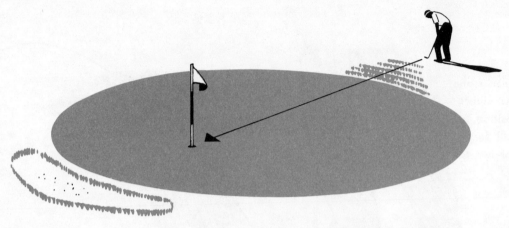

Using putter from off the green,
with the grass around the edge
of the green smooth and cut
fairly close

Don't overdo your putting shot from off the green. Once they discover how effective this shot can be, many players use it indiscriminately. Be sure your situation resembles the one outlined above.

SHANKING: When you shank, you hit the ball at the juncture of the shaft and the clubhead known as the shank.

Usually the shaft and clubhead contact the ball on the inside (right side) of the shaft so that it spins off to the right. If the clubface makes secondary contact, the ball will fly off to the right at about a 45-degree angle in what is known as a semi-shank.

At other times the shank catches the ball, and the clubface doesn't make contact. This is what happens on those shots that are almost at right angles to the intended line of flight.

Whether the shot is a semi-shank or a full shank, the results are equally horrible. More often than not, you'll add a stroke to your score and end up in a worse spot than you were before.

The shank results when the shaft rather than the clubhead meets the ball. Examine the shank and you'll see what I mean. (Most shanks take place with the irons, as you can see by comparing their clubheads with the woods.)

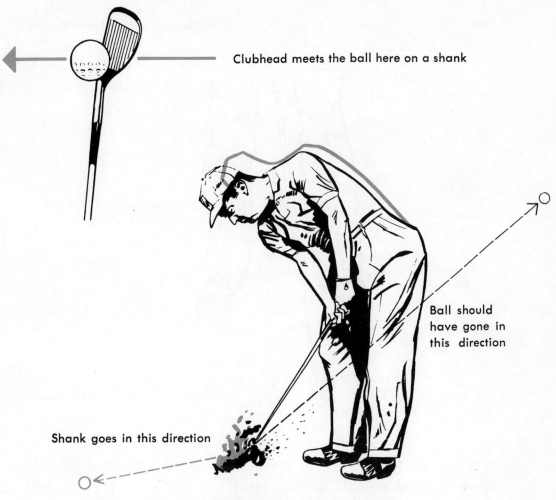

Clubhead meets the ball here on a shank

Ball should have gone in this direction

Shank goes in this direction

Incorrect: Body has rocked forward from the force of the swing, causing a shank

When you shank, the plane of the swing moves out because (*1*) your body has rocked forward or (*2*) your hands have moved out.

Shanks on a full power swing take place when centrifugal force pulls the body forward. That's why your weight should be centered through the heels as the swing gets under way, the basic cure for this shanking fault.

If you are a chronic shanker on full shots, you should address the ball well out on the toe of the club and exaggerate centering your weight through the heels. These remedies will help correct your habit of rocking forward on the downswing.

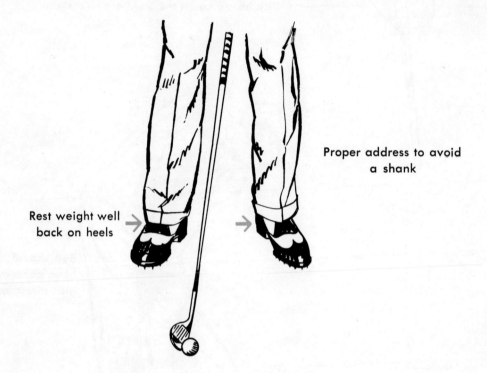

Rest weight well
back on heels

Proper address to avoid
a shank

These corrective measures should be temporary. The best place to
cure the shank is on the practice tee. If you try to cure it on the golf
course, the rest of your game is bound to suffer. You can't play decent
golf is you're concentrating on avoiding a shank.

INSIDE SHANK

To understand the shank that usually takes place on swings in which
you don't use your full power, swing a short iron back well inside a
parallel line extending back from the ball. Note that this type of backswing moves your right elbow *behind* your right hip.

Now, to swing the club back and then hit the ball, your right elbow
has got to be *ahead of the right hip*. Therefore, it must go up and *out*,
lifting the plane of the swing out. This frequently results in the shank.

This is another of those golfing errors that often take place in the
very act of correction. You begin to feel that you can avoid the shank
by keeping the swing in close. You swing more and more inside. You

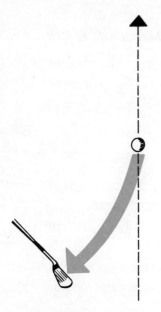

Swing short iron back well inside the intended line of flight

Plane of the swing is forced outward, causing a shank

Cure for the shank: Take the clubhead straight back from the ball

keep shanking. It's awful! I once saw a player almost completely encircle a green with four straight shanks. He kept aiming toward the pin, and the ball kept squirting out to the right. He began the series on his third shot and played his seventh from about 50 feet to the left of where he started. I don't think he even realized what a ludicrous performance was taking place.

You must take the clubhead straight back from the ball so that your right elbow will move only slightly away from your body. Then it will be inside your hip so that you can bring the clubhead into the ball square. Make the backswing loose and free—a good way to overcome the tightening that makes you hug your body with your arms on the backswing.

This cure may seem a little risky at first, but there's no alternative.

SUMMARY

I've dealt separately with the two basic causes of shanking so that you can understand them better. At times, however, both are responsible for the same shot; each can easily augment the other to produce the shank. While I have linked the forward rocking error to the full shot and the shank caused by the inside swing to the shorter shot, there are instances when both forces are at work. So whatever shanking you do, look for both causes.

See HEELING.

SIDEHILL LIES: When the ball is below your feet, there's a great danger of shanking. The tendency is to pitch forward during the swing. Thus the plane of the swing slides out and you hit the ball in the neck (shank) of the club (*see* SHANKING).

Your best countermeasure is to keep your weight back on your heels throughout the swing. Also, swing well within your maximum power so you can stay on balance.

Since you must stand nearer the ball on this shot to reach it, your swing will be more upright. Thus you'll tend to push the shot to the

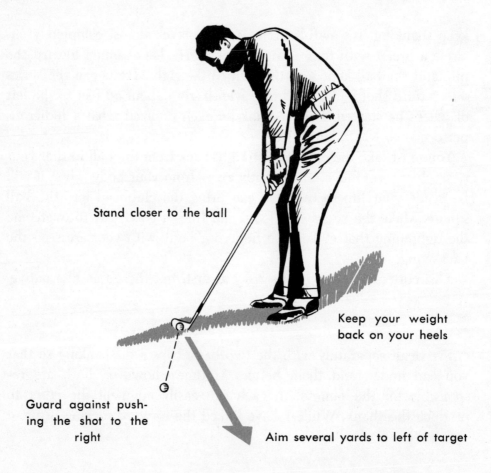

Stand closer to the ball

Keep your weight back on your heels

Guard against pushing the shot to the right

Aim several yards to left of target

Aim to right
of target

Stand farther
from the ball

With this sidehill lie, it is all but
impossible to keep from pulling
or hooking the shot, so aim to
the right and play for a pull
hook

right. You can counteract this tendency by aiming several yards to the left of your target.

On the other sidehill lie the ball is on a higher level than your feet. The tendency in this situation is to pull the shot strongly to the left. You must stand farther away from the ball to adjust to this shot. The resultant flattened (roundhouse) swing is natural for pulls and hooks.

Since it is almost impossible to keep from pulling or hooking (or both) on this shot, the best solution is to aim to the right and play for the pull-hook.

Be careful not to fall away from the ball. If you do, you'll hit it well out on the toe of the club. At best, you'll lose needed power; at the worst, you may hit the ball so far out on the toe that it will shoot out to the right like a shanked shot.

SKYING THE BALL: The skied shot in golf is roughly analagous to the high pop fly in baseball. Both result from hitting the ball too much on the underside.

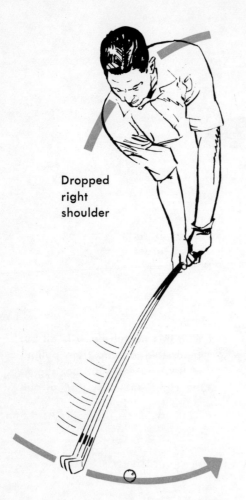

Dropped
right
shoulder

Skying the ball

Ball teed too high

You can sky the ball when you drop your right shoulder during the downswing. This lowers the plane of the swing so that the clubhead contacts the ball too much on the underside.

The right shoulder drops when you make the mistake of trying to add power to your swing. You can remedy this error by hitting well within your maximum power, letting the body's recoil and your hand action produce the needed clubhead speed.

You also sky with the driver when you tee the ball too high. The ball should be teed just high enough to permit the whole clubface to contact all of the ball without touching the ground—just a shade to spare.

Duck your head as the downswing begins, and you'll sky the ball. Again, you're trying to add power that should come naturally. Use the same remedy you would for lowering the right shoulder.

See SCLAFFING.

SKYWRITING: *See* LOOPING AT THE TOP

SLICE: A right-handed player curves the ball to the right because he puts a left-to-right spin on it. The most frequent way of imparting this spin is to bring the clubhead *across* the ball from right to left. The other method is to slant the clubface out. Combine both techniques, and you can produce an even bigger slice.

When you're slicing deliberately, here are some points to keep in mind:

(*1*) The simplest method is to hit the ball with a normal swing but the clubface open. Grip the club *after* you've adjusted the clubface. Otherwise you'll automatically readjust the clubface during the swing.

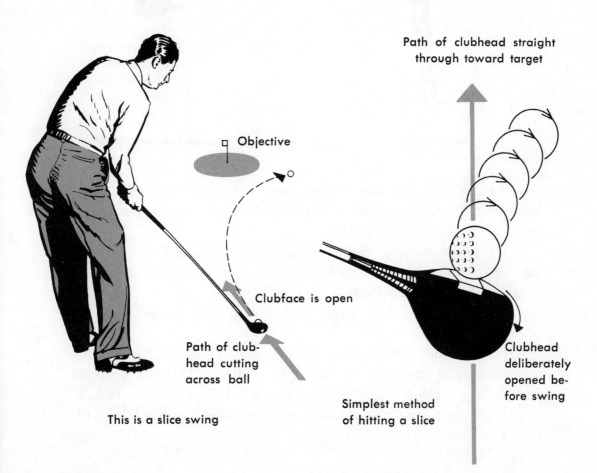

Path of clubhead straight through toward target

Objective

Clubface is open

Path of club-head cutting across ball

This is a slice swing

Clubhead deliberately opened before swing

Simplest method of hitting a slice

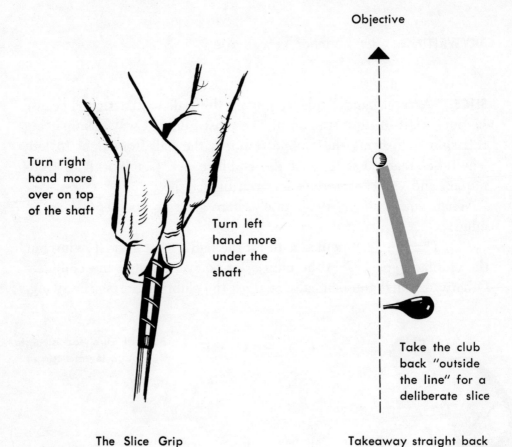

Objective

Turn right
hand more
over on top
of the shaft

Turn left
hand more
under the
shaft

Take the club
back "outside
the line" for a
deliberate slice

The Slice Grip   Takeaway straight back

(2) Place your left hand farther under the shaft and your right hand over it more. See that the V's formed by thumb and forefinger point just to the left of the chin.

(3) In order to bring the clubhead across the ball from right to left (or outside in), take it back along that same line. This is known as taking the club back "outside the line."

(4) You can slice more easily with a club with a small amount of loft.

(5) Finish your slicing swing with the palm of your left hand down and (naturally) the palm of your right hand up. This will prevent hand rolling, making you close the clubface before you hit the ball.

(6) The open stance (right foot advanced ahead of the left) will help you slice.

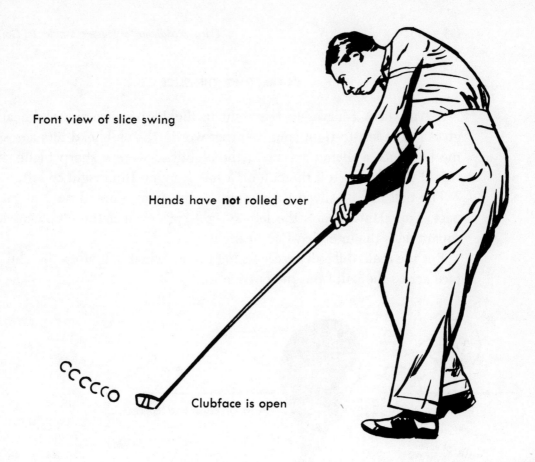

Front view of slice swing

Hands have **not** rolled over

Clubface is open

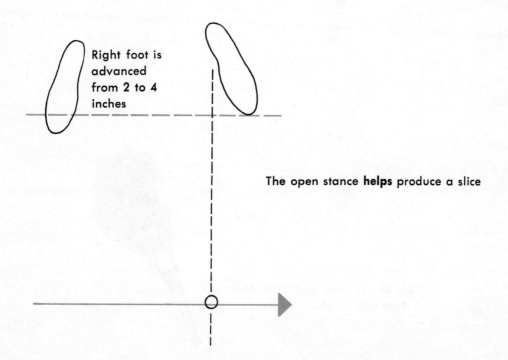

Right foot is
advanced
from 2 to 4
inches

The open stance **helps** produce a slice

CORRECTING THE SLICE

A ball slices (curves to the right in flight) because the clubhead gives it that left-to-right spin. In other words, the clubhead hits across the ball with a slicing action. If the clubhead were a sharp blade, it would slice a piece off the ball on a line running from right to left.

The ball will be sliced if the clubface is open (slanted out) at impact. This slant imparts the left-to-right spin even if the clubhead is square with the intended line of flight.

But the main difficulty with slicing occurs when you whip the clubface across the ball from the outside in.

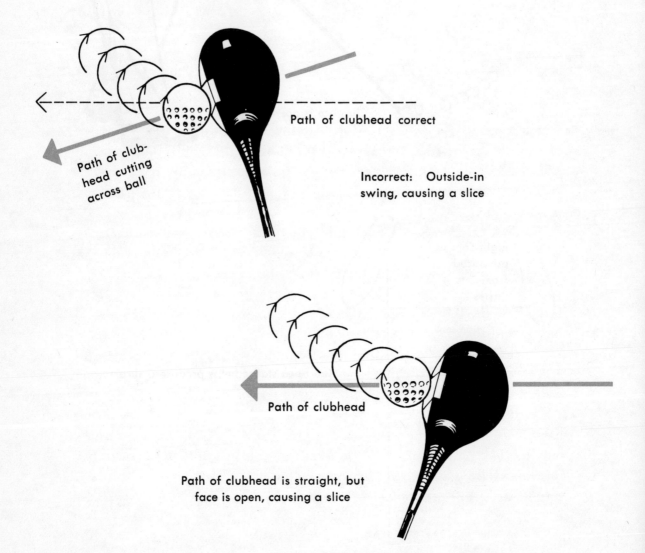

Path of clubhead correct

Path of clubhead cutting across ball

Incorrect: Outside-in swing, causing a slice

Path of clubhead

Path of clubhead is straight, but face is open, causing a slice

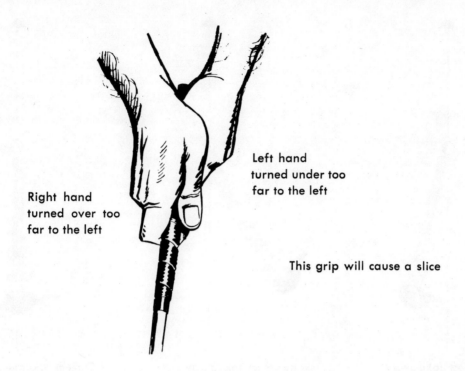

Right hand
turned over too
far to the left

Left hand
turned under too
far to the left

This grip will cause a slice

Slicing adds much to the problem of control, but it is the extent to which it cuts down on distance that makes it the great natural enemy of the golfer. When your clubhead goes across the ball rather than squarely into it, you lose a lot of power. Furthermore, to reach a given point, the slice has to travel a greater distance than the straight ball so that some of your power is wasted.

The first place to look for trouble is the grip. Maybe your left hand is in too weak a position: *i.e.*, it may be too far left. As we saw in the section on GRIP, the left hand grip should be in such a position that you can see two knuckles when you look down at address. The V formed by the thumb and first finger of the left hand should be pointing toward the chin.

This left hand position is best for most golfers, though some require a firmer grip in which the left hand is turned over more to the right so that you can see part of the third (ring) finger knuckle.

Check your right hand grip next. You may be turning the right hand over too far to the left. You should be able to look down and see only the first (index finger) knuckle of the right hand. If the back of the hand shows more than knuckle, you'll know it's over too far. Just turn it back so you see only that one knuckle.

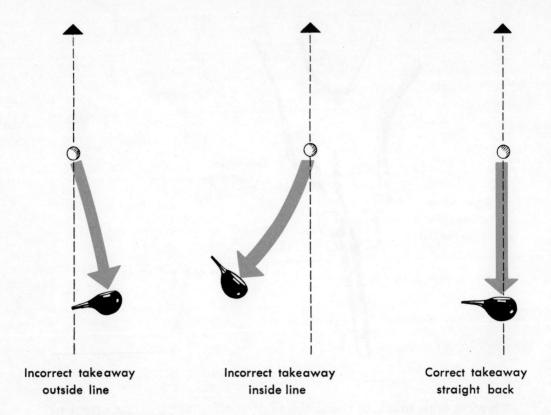

Incorrect takeaway
outside line

Incorrect takeaway
inside line

Correct takeaway
straight back

No more drastic adjustment of the hands is necessary. Should the slice persist, look elsewhere for the trouble.

The swing fault that causes the slice may occur during the takeaway. If you take the club back outside the line, you are likely to bring it back into the ball along the same path and cut across it for a slice.

If you take the club back inside the line, you'll run into the old hip and elbow trouble and cut across the ball from the outside.

Take the club back straight.

If the grip and takeaway are approximately right and you continue to slice, you may not be turning your body enough on the backswing so that the right elbow ends up behind the right hip.

Even with a fundamentally correct backswing, you can still slice the shot if your body and hands get too far ahead of the clubhead on the downswing. This faulty action takes place when you shift your body forward at the start of the downswing instead of shifting your weight to the left and simply unwinding your body in the course of the swing.

If the slice is your nemesis, study the sections on GRIP, BACKSWING and DOWNSWING in relation to the above-mentioned faults.

Incorrect: The right elbow
is behind the right hip

Incorrect: Not enough body
turn on backswing

Body and hands too far
ahead of clubhead

Clubface open, causing a slice

SPOON: *See* CLUBS

SPRAYING: We've all experienced "one of those days" when we hit the ball all over the lot. Spraying can be more frustrating than slicing when it dogs you for eighteen holes. When you know you're slicing, you can take preventive measures to avoid serious trouble on the right. But when you're having a wild time, all you can do is take the consequences.

Obviously, there's no specific cure for general wildness, as there is when your off-line shots follow a particular pattern, but you ought to check the positioning of the ball, particularly if you seem to be swinging the same way each time and getting different results.

Many players are careless about positioning the ball. They try to line up with the general direction of the hole and let fly. You can swing correctly at the ball and still hit it far off the intended line if you position the ball incorrectly. If the ball is wrongly positioned, you won't hit it at the bottom of your swing arc.

On wild days you usually begin by positioning the ball the wrong way. Then you overcompensate on the next shot and never succeed in getting lined up correctly.

STANCE: The term stance includes the placement of the feet, the distribution of weight, the extent to which the knees should be flexed or bent, the position of the hips and posterior, the posture of the back, the position of the head and the position of the arms with reference to each other.

PLACING THE FEET

For the full drive, the feet should be about as far apart as the shoulders are wide. You should have the feeling that the feet are directly under the shoulders. The left toe should be turned out at about a 30 degree angle, the right toe at about a 10 degree angle.

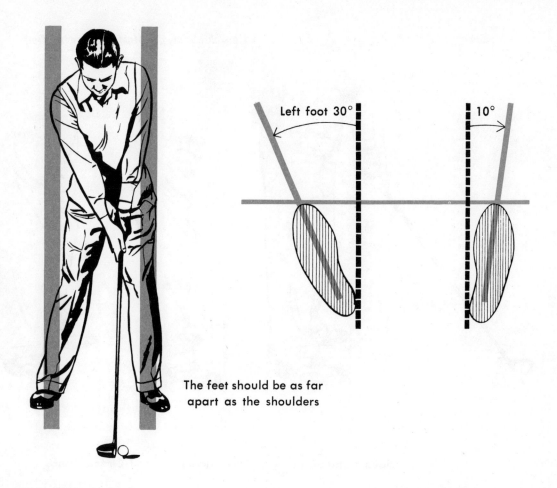

Left foot 30°   10°

The feet should be as far
apart as the shoulders

These specifications may seem a bit arbitrary, but they are based on much experience and no little experimenting. In placing your feet for the drive, you are seeking a compromise position between a balanced stance of sufficient width and enough freedom of movement for sufficient body rotation. The wider the stance, the more solidly you will be planted, and you want to be solidly planted. The narrower the stance, the more easily you will be able to turn the hips going back, and you want to be able to turn the hips freely on the backswing. The foot placement described above combines these two ideals to the greatest effect.

This stance for the driver should be square: *i.e.*, your feet should be on a line with each other. A line starting from the tip of the left toe and parallel to the line of flight would touch the tip of the right toe. An open stance is one in which the right foot is withdrawn about two or three inches from this imaginary line paralleling the intended

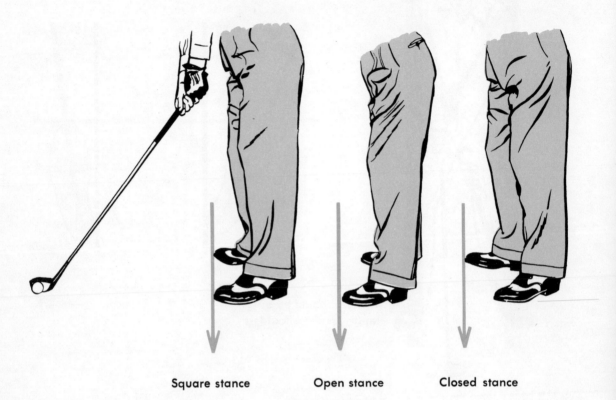

Square stance   Open stance   Closed stance

line of flight. A closed stance is just the opposite—the left foot is with-drawn about two or three inches from this line. The uses of these stances will be taken up later in this section.

The stance for the driver is the basic one. The stance for shots with the other clubs call for minor variations in the placement of the feet (*see* CLUBS).

WEIGHT DISTRIBUTION

When you've positioned your feet for the driver stance, take care that a slight preponderance of your body weight rests between the balls of your feet and the heels. The natural force emanating from the downswing tends to pull the body slightly forward. Unless re-sisted, this forward pull can make you strike the ball with the heel of

Slight preponderance of body weight

the club so that you lose power and direction. If you are pulled too far forward, you may shank a shot by hitting the ball with the neck or hosel of the club so that it shoots out to the right almost at a right angle.

This problem of weight distribution at address suggests another of the many compromises you must make to develop a proper golf swing. If your weight is too far back over the heels, you'll end up with a flat-footed swing that will usually send your shot too far to the left. But remember, only a "slight preponderance" of weight is necessary; don't overdo it.

When you start your swing for full shots, keep your weight evenly on both feet. For short shots, put a little more weight on the left foot at the start of your stroke.

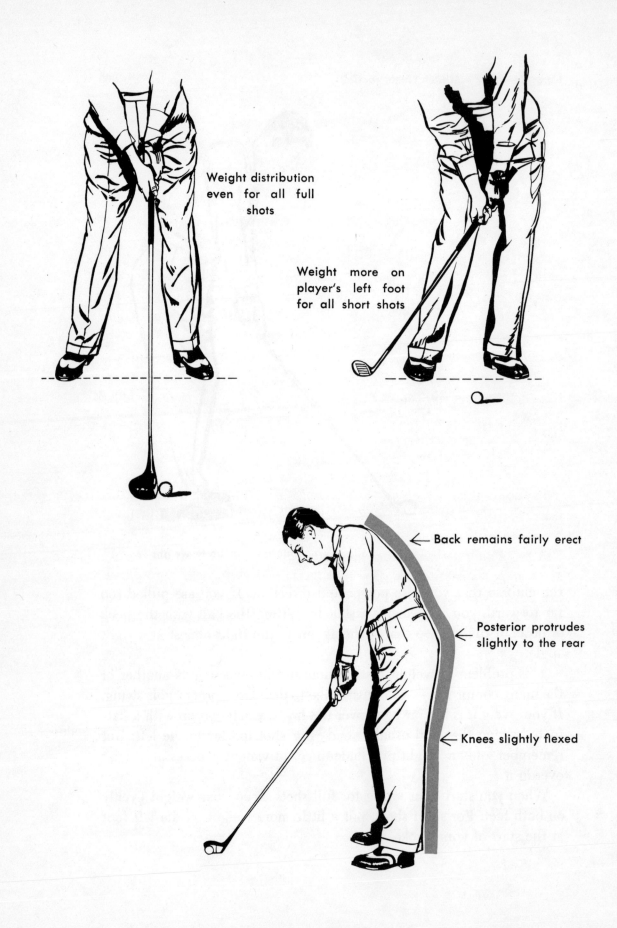

Weight distribution even for all full shots

Weight more on player's left foot for all short shots

← Back remains fairly erect

← Posterior protrudes slightly to the rear

← Knees slightly flexed

FLEXING THE KNEES

Your knees should be flexed or slightly bent when you stand to the ball. This helps relax the leg muscles.

HIPS AND POSTERIOR AT ADDRESS

Your butt should protrude slightly to the rear as you stand to the ball, which means that your hips will move back a little. With your hips out of the way, your arms and elbows are not obstructed on the downswing. This slight adjustment in stance can save you many sliced or topped shots—the result of the right hip blocking the right elbow on the downswing. (The elbow must move out and around the hip, thereby raising the plane of your swing slightly so that you are forced to swing *across* the ball from the outside—*i.e.*, right to left.) The "cane seat" stance allows your arms more freedom.

BACK POSTURE

In the proper stance your back should be erect, though arched forward slightly so that you may reach the ball comfortably. But don't bend forward too much.

A crouching position is no good for golf. It tenses the muscles, it's awkward and it prevents your hitting the ball with maximum effect. Moreover, when you're crouched at the start, you tend to straighten up a bit while the swing is underway. This is one of the major causes of topped shots.

Correct posture at address   Incorrect stance   Incorrect posture

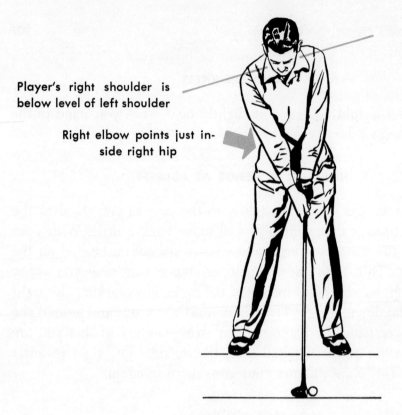

Player's right shoulder is below level of left shoulder

Right elbow points just inside right hip

SHOULDER POSITION

In the correct stance, the right shoulder will be slightly below the level of the left. This is because you must drop the right hand below the left in order to grip the club. The space between shoulder levels is really the distance your right hand must drop to be in the correct position on the grip.

If the shoulders were level, you would have to stretch the right arm unnaturally. Your right arm should be in a relaxed position at address with the elbow pointing just inside the hip, where it should remain until just before the ball is hit.

HEAD POSITION

Your head should be so positioned in the stance that it remains still throughout the swing and after the ball is well on its way.

If you are of normal build, I strongly urge you to hold your head so that your eyes are directly over the ball. I do not subscribe to the theory that the head should be cocked slightly to the right so that the left eye is on the back of the ball.

In the ideal swing, both eyes should be on the ball while the head is centered. The head should remain in this position between address and contact.

I would make an exception here for players who are very compactly built with broad shoulders and short neck. These golfers will find it helpful to cock the head slightly to the right before beginning the swing. Then the left shoulder can make the turn necessary to complete the backswing without disturbing the position of the hands.

Head straight and centered

Compactly built players should cock head slightly to the right

ARM EXTENSION AND POSITION

When you stand correctly in relation to the ball, your arms are comfortably extended. You don't feel that you are reaching for the ball or standing over it.

This feeling of comfortable extension determines the distance you stand from the ball. Because no two golfers are built alike, I can only stress this individual feeling of comfort and "rightness." You should sense that your arms are so extended that you can deliver a maximum blow.

The left arm and the shaft of the club should form a straight line extending from the left shoulder to the ball. The left elbow should point toward your left side pocket.

Your right arm should be more relaxed and bent at the elbow than the left. And your right elbow should point just inside the right hip.

The elbows should be as close together as is comfortably possible, though you should never force them together.

When the elbows are comfortably close, your right elbow is inside the hip and close to the body—right where it should be during the swing.

See ADDRESS TO THE BALL, DRIVING *and* PUTTING.

STEERING: When you steer, you ease up on the swing and "wish" it along. Anxiety, lack of confidence—call it what you will—the only answer is to prepare for the shot in advance by thinking it through with confidence.

STRATEGY: Specific situations and solutions are given under CLUBS, SAND TRAPS, SCORING RANGE, TOURNAMENTS and WIND. For general discussions of strategy see DRIVING, PSYCHOLOGY OF GOLF and PUTTING.

SWAYING: Swaying is the fault generally associated with pushing or pulling, but it can also cause other faults such as topping, hitting behind the ball, slicing and hooking.

Left arm is straighter with elbow pointing toward left pocket

Player's right arm is more relaxed, with elbow just inside right hip

Head and
body have
swayed back
off line

Hands have
rolled over,
causing the
clubhead to
close

Clubhead is
ahead of the
hands at
impact

Head and
body have
swayed for-
ward off line

Clubhead is
behind hands
at impact

Clubface is open

Incorrect sway back from
the ball, causing a pull or
a hook

Incorrect sway forward
from the ball, causing a
push or a slice

The sway is simply a lateral movement of the body—either backward or forward—during the course of the swing. This fault moves
your head away from the ball and places your body in a different position from the address alignment.

When your head moves, you'll top the shot or hit behind the ball.
If you sway away from the ball, as usually happens on the backswing,
you'll very likely pull or hook the ball. Following a sway on the backswing, you'll bring the clubhead into the ball ahead of your hands
and pull the ball. And if your hands roll over, as they are likely to do
in this case, the shot will be a combination pull and hook.

If you sway forward, your hands will come in ahead of the clubhead and you'll push. Also, this faulty action will leave the clubface
open so that you'll slice as well as push.

The cure? Rotate your body on the backswing, head firmly in place, and unwind it on the downswing, head still firmly in place.

Sometimes a golfer can offset a backward sway with a forward one, a rare occurrence equivalent to getting away with murder.

See BACKSWING, DOWNSWING *and* STANCE.

SWING (GENERAL): In the separate sections on swing components, I have dissected the golf swing so that you can understand every phase involved. If you have some recurring fault, I want you to be able to turn to the proper section and find a basic reason for it. If you have a particular trouble on a particular day, I want you to be able to find its underlying cause.

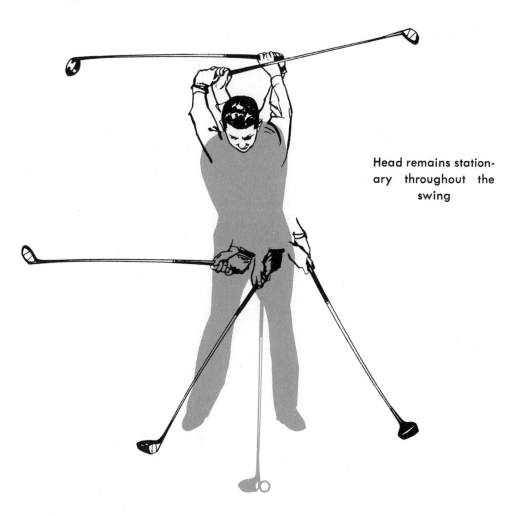

Head remains stationary throughout the swing

What I emphatically do *not* want to do is leave you with the impression that the golf swing is a complicated and confusing mass of separate movements and details. It is not. It is—or should be—a simple thing, enabling you to get your hands in the proper position to deliver a hard, square blow against the ball with the clubface moving truly along the intended line of flight.

The various parts of the golf swing must be understood before the whole can be reduced to its simplest terms. In taking up the parts of the swing point by point, I have simply tried to give you a better understanding of it. I do *not* suggest that you can hit a golf ball properly while thinking of the act in terms of dozens of separate parts and details.

Let's try to take the swing apart and then put it back together into a simple, one-piece affair.

To give you a central idea to cling to as you pursue this section, let me state my definition of a good golf swing. A good golf swing is one that brings the clubhead into the hitting area at maximum speed square with the intended line of flight and continues square along that line until well after the ball is met and is on its way.

If you can bring the clubhead square with the intended line of flight so that it travels parallel with the ground four inches before the ball is met and make it continue square along the line for four inches past the ball, then you have a good swing. And if you can add an inch on each side of the ball, thereby increasing your margin for error, you'll have a much better swing.

This explains why players with very bad swings can occasionally hit a very good golf shot. Now and then such players will catch the ball just right, even though their best swings bring the clubhead square to the line of flight and an inch or less behind the ball. But with such a small margin for error, good shots will be few and far between. There can be no consistency. Also, the poorer shots of the player with the good swing will be less disastrous than those of the player with the bad swing.

Watch a really good swinger some time. Notice that when the clubhead is a foot or two away from the ball, you get the impression that this swinger is certain to make a good shot. The bad swinger's good shots are obviously accidental.

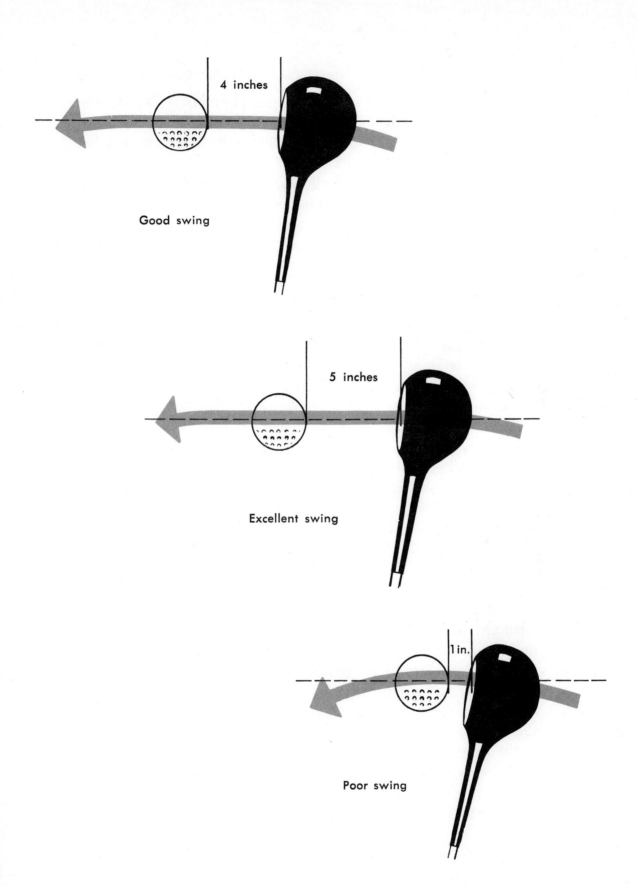

4 inches

Good swing

5 inches

Excellent swing

1 in.

Poor swing

Watch one of the tournaments on the professional circuit. The swings you see will look different. But in all of them the clubface will be square to the ball early and will remain that way for several inches past the ball along the line of flight.

That's the objective of the golf swing you should keep in mind.

As stated in my earlier book, *Advanced Golf*, any sound golf game must be based on the principle of simplicity. The more complicated the swing, the less consistent your game, which is likely to break down during crucial moments.

I like to think of the backswing as simply a means of getting the hands in the proper position to hit and of the downswing as a means for clubbing the ball square to the line of flight at maximum speed. But I also like to think of both backswing and downswing as parts of a single action.

The swing is an inclusive operation that begins the moment you start sizing up the shot.

You start by picturing the kind of shot you want to make and the technique you will use. Some people apparently think that a golfer who isn't very good should think only in terms of getting the ball airborne in the general direction of the hole. But there are no half measures in golf. Besides, it costs nothing to strive for perfection. And in the end you will score better on a particular day and improve your game over the long haul.

Some may say that golf is just a game and should be played for the simple enjoyment it affords without making a lot of hard work out of it. Don't you believe it! Such an attitude toward golf is fit for the buzzards! Sure, there's a certain amount of pleasure in just beating the ball around, but there's a lot more pleasure in really trying to play the game right—for all it is worth. So do your best on every shot.

The ideal golf swing varies as little as possible from shot to shot and can be depended upon to produce the same or similar results time after time.

The hands play the most important part in the golf swing. The whole purpose of your backswing movements is to get your hands into the proper position to deliver the blow. On the downswing, you are bringing power to bear on a strike executed by the hands, and in order that your hands can operate properly, you've got to get your body out of the way.

Given the opportunity, the hands will nearly always do what they should. We use our hands so often in our daily lives that they are very well trained.

Think of the swing as a single action. But if you feel that a specific function is fouling up the works, check over these swing components to see what the trouble might be.

The main components of the golf swing are discussed separately under BACKSWING, DOWNSWING and FINISH OF THE SWING.

For a detailed treatment of the recommended swing for each club, see CLUBS.

Individual swings for the various strokes are described under DRIVING, PUTTING and SCORING RANGE.

T

TAKEAWAY: *See* BACKSWING

TEE SHOT: *See* DRIVING

THREE-QUARTER SHOT: *See* SCORING RANGE

TOEING: Some golfers won't believe that the built-in loft of the clubface can lift the ball up to the right height and send it on its way. They seem to feel that they must give the clubface an assist with their hands. These are the golfers who most often hit the ball on the toe of the club.

Faulty hand action induces a falling away from the ball so that the plane of the swing is drawn inward and the toe connects. The result is a considerable loss of power and therefore distance. As in the case of heeling, your full weight is missing behind the clubhead. A shot

Weight
on right
leg

Incorrect: Falling
away from ball,
which draws the
plane of the swing
inward, causing ball
to be hit on the toe of
the club

hit out on the toe but still on the clubface proper will travel fairly straight. But if the error is pronounced, you'll hit the ball so far out on the toe that it may go off almost at right angles, resembling that awful shank in flight.

This fault almost always stems from keeping the weight back on the right foot during the downswing. Actually, it's a departure from the basic fundamentals of the swing, which call for shifting the weight from the right to the left side as soon as you begin the downswing. This weight shift is essential to hitting down and through the ball or in the case of the drive, hitting through the ball with a level sweep. If you keep your weight back on your right foot, you'll try to hit the ball with an upward sweep, and this is no good.

If you put too much effort into the swing and lose your balance, you're likely to fall away from the ball. Then if you hit the ball at all, you'll toe it.

To overcome hitting the ball on the toe of the club (*1*) shift your weight to the left side at the start of the downswing, and (*2*) swing within your maximum power.

See HEELING.

TOPPING: Among the troubles that beset the high-handicap golfer, one of the most frequent and annoying is hitting the ball on top.

Straightening up the body during the swing is the most frequent cause of topping. Perhaps you are too anxious to see the ball on its way so you raise your head. That is topping in its simplest form.

When you crouch too much at address, you're likely to top. This error is particularly insidious because so many players adopt the faulty

Incorrect: Too-crouched position at address

position expressly to avoid topping. The player crouches because he thinks he'll stay down on the shot, but during the swing he straightens up a bit to take a full, free swing.

This straightening action naturally raises the plane of the swing so that the clubhead meets the ball on top with the result that the ball dribbles only a few yards toward the hole.

You may, of course, raise up slightly during the swing, even though your position at address may have been fairly erect and in conformity with the basic stance. And this fault must be included among the causes of topping. Yet the danger is far greater when you are crouched over the ball at address.

RIGHT ELBOW

I have seen golfers go along topping shot after shot while at the same time staying fairly well down on the shot and keeping their heads

Incorrect: Player hitting from a crouched position. Black dotted line shows plane of swing if the player had stayed in his original crouch. Green dotted line shows how player has straightened up a little during the swing, raising the plane, causing a "top."

Original position of ball

Incorrect: Right elbow is away from body and outside right hip, causing outside-in swing, and plane of swing to go upward and outward (green dotted line)

The player is hitting the ball on top and also on the heel of the club

quite still throughout the swing. This always mystifies the topper, who says to himself, "I know I kept my head down, and still I top the ball!" What happens is that the right elbow flies away from the body and moves outside the right hip.

From that position you must swing from the outside in (across the ball from right to left) in order to make contact. When the right elbow goes up and out, the plane of the swing is tilted upward and outward. Thus you end up hitting the ball on top with the heel of the club.

When your topped shots take off to the left—out under the left arm as it were—you may be sure you're not positioning your right elbow correctly. Keep the right elbow tucked in close to the body. It should be pointing to the ground until the downswing has begun, and the right hip should be turned enough so that the right elbow will stay inside (or in front of) it.

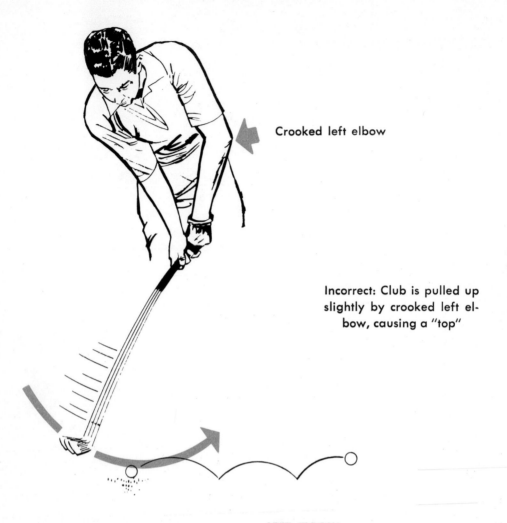

Crooked left elbow

Incorrect: Club is pulled up slightly by crooked left elbow, causing a "top"

LEFT ELBOW

A frequent cause of topping, particularly with the shorter irons, is crooking the left elbow just before impact. You try to lift the ball with your arms and hands instead of hitting down through it and letting the loft of the club raise it.

Remember that the left arm is straight at address and remains straight throughout the backswing and until after the ball is hit. It's fatal to try to lift the ball with your hands and absolutely contrary to the basic principles of hitting a golf ball.

BALL POSITION

Faulty positioning of the ball in relation to the feet at address is another cause of topping. Each club reaches a point at the bottom of the swing arc (*see* ADDRESS TO THE BALL *and* CLUBS). If you place the ball too far back toward the right foot at address and fail to compensate for this fault during the swing, you won't reach the bottom of your arc by the time the club-head reaches the ball. You'll top the shot because the clubhead will still be too high to contact the ball in the center. You can correct this fault by simply placing the ball at address as outlined in ADDRESS TO THE BALL.

TOPPING CURES

The cures for topping the ball can be listed as follows:

(1) Keep your head still throughout the swing.

(2) Maintain an erect and comfortable posture at address. A position that's too crouched tends to cramp the muscles, and you are likely to straighten up involuntarily during the swing to obtain freedom of movement.

Faulty ball positioning too far back, causing a "top"

Ball should be positioned here

(3) Keep the right elbow tucked into the body and pointing down until just before the ball is hit and always inside (to the left of) the right hip.

(4) Let the clubhead do the lifting; don't consciously try to lift the ball. Keep your left arm straight but not rigid until after impact.

(5) Position the ball properly at address so that you naturally reach the bottom of the swing arc *at* the ball.

TOURNAMENTS: Tournaments here means every kind of tournament. The problems faced by golfers playing in the tenth flight consolation of the club tournament and in the big professional events are essentially alike.

The same tactical problems arise in both tournament and informal play. However, many golfers who use sound strategy in their informal

game fail miserably in tournament competitions. (The reverse is not the case.) That's why I've related the following problems of strategy and tactics in tournament play: *

Situation: Your opponent is one whom you figure to beat easily. Should you relax or go after him right from the start?

Solution: When you enter a tournament, you're in it to win. So knuckle down. There's plenty of time to be friendly after the match is over.

Situation: You are playing a strong favorite and figure to lose on the basis of past performances. Are you going to take long chances from the outset in an effort to bring about an upset?

Solution: Play your own game to the best of your ability. Take chances when circumstances warrant them; play safe when that seems best. Too many players with little tournament experience try to decide who's going to win the match before it begins. Then they play accordingly. Against the odds-on favorite, they'll shoot the works (on the theory that they've nothing to lose), and so they'll hand over the match to the favorite on a silver platter. Play your own game. That's your best chance to win.

Situation: It would appear that your opponent is about to make a bogey. You are in good position for simple par. It is match play.

Solution: Don't take any unnecessary chances or you may wind up with a double bogey and less a hole you should have won. Then you'll be two holes worse off than you thought you were going to be. If we assume that the match has been even, you'll leave the green one down instead of one up. And it takes a minimum of two holes to go from one down to one up (which is why they're known as "vice versa holes").

Situation: Your opponent or partner has broken a rule.

Solution: Call it to his attention politely but firmly. You're not out to avail yourself of every possible technicality, but golf rules should be observed. If in match play you permit your opponent to get away

---

* In order to differentiate between "strategy" and "tactics," you may consider these terms in their military application—*i.e.*, "strategy" refers to a broad plan that includes various tactical moves, whereas "tactics" concerns individual plays and problems and their method of execution.

with an infraction, you're a poor sportsman. If he's in a tournament, he should know the rules and follow them. If you break a rule unwittingly, call it on yourself and take the penalty. If your opponent reminds you of an infraction with which you were unfamiliar, accept his pointer with good grace. When in doubt, always consult the referee or the rule book before proceeding.

Situation: Your match or medal round is about to begin.

Solution: Be sure you have everything you need—tees, plenty of balls, all your clubs within the regulation limit, umbrella and rain equipment if the weather is in the least threatening, rule book, scorecard, and pencil. Then brief your caddy on what you expect from him. If you intend to ask his advice from time to time, tell him so. If you want to make up your own mind without assistance, let him know it. And if you want him to stick with you or stay ahead with the ball, explain as much before you start out.

Once these preliminaries are settled, you can concentrate strictly on playing golf.

Situation: Your opponent's putt is very near the hole. Should you concede it?

Solution: Are you sure he can make it? If so, you might concede. If not, make him putt. Maybe he's already given you a longer putt. No matter—short as it is, his putt may be tougher. And possibly he's given you a fairly longish one or two to make you putt a short one later on, counting on the element of surprise to upset you. Remember,

If you're not absolutely sure your opponent can sink a short putt, then make him putt it.

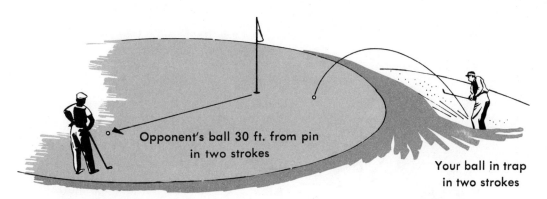

Opponent's ball 30 ft. from pin
in two strokes

Your ball in trap
in two strokes

Get that ball out of the trap, onto the
green. Try to get inside your opponent.
Keep the pressure on him. Don't ever
give a hole away without trying your
very best to at least tie it.

he's not obliged to concede you a putt or vice versa. You are competitors; there is no question of courtesy. Let your opponent know you mean business. Make him work for it and expect him to treat you the same way. That's just golf.

Situation: You are in sand or rough near the green. Your opponent is on the green about 30 feet away and is even with you on strokes. The flag is close to the edge of the green, and there's not much room from your position. It's a risky shot if you're going to get close.

Solution: Get that ball on the green inside of your opponent. Don't make things easy for him by taking a long chance and failing to get on at all. He may three-putt, and you may hole your putt. Never give a hole away if you can tie it. The long chance is okay if you can leave yourself with a tying putt. Keep the pressure on.

Situation: You're faced with a short putt in a match or medal tournament.

Solution: Don't make a major operation out of a simple play. Line up the putt and tap it in. If you take too much time over short putts, you're likely to tense up until eventually you'll miss one.

Situation: You've fallen well behind in the early stages of the match. Should you begin to take long chances?

Solution: Steady on. Each player can expect a certain number of breaks, and the good and the bad usually even up. Sometimes everything will go your way in the early stages, and you'll build up a quick

Do not take **too** much time on short putts. This usually builds up tension and may cause you to miss the putt.

lead. But if you're behind, don't be discouraged. Your breaks may be on the way, so keep playing, and you'll be ready to take advantage of them. Don't take any unnecessary risks in an attempt to create breaks for yourself. But show your best golf.

Situation: You have a commanding lead. Your problem is to protect it.

Strategy: The best way to protect a lead in a golf match is to add to it. Don't try to halve the remaining holes to close out the match. You may slump, and your opponent may rally. Keep in top form until the match is over.

Situation: Your match-lay opponent has gone out of bounds from the tee.

Solution: Play it safe. If you're afraid of going out of bounds too, use an iron instead of your driver. Some players feel that it's only sporting to take chances in this situation. But that's not golf.

Situation: The last round of medal play competition is coming up. You need an exceptional score to qualify or place in the prize list.

Solution: Steady on. Don't try to force your breaks too much. Play your own best game as you would in match play against a superior opponent.

TROUBLE SHOTS: In general, trouble shots may be described as those which are hit fairly well on the clubface but go in the wrong direction. Some of these shots (the slices and hooks) curve off line in the course of their flight. Others (the pushes and pulls) start off in the wrong direction and continue that way.

The slice and hook can be valuable weapons in certain situations, as when a tree blocks a straight path to the hole. The safer course is usually the wise one, but occasionally you'll have to "go for broke." When a tree stands athwart your path to the hole, a hook or a slice may come in handy. If you can't get around that tree, perhaps you can skim under or climb over its branches. The low skimmer can be helpful when you can't pitch to an elevated green. You may be able to run a low shot up the bank to the green or bounce it up and over from the bank.

Here are some valuable pointers on trouble-shooting:

(*1*) High shots and slices go together. If you need height on your shot as well as a curve, choose the slice instead of the hook. It's easier to raise the ball with a slice than a hook.

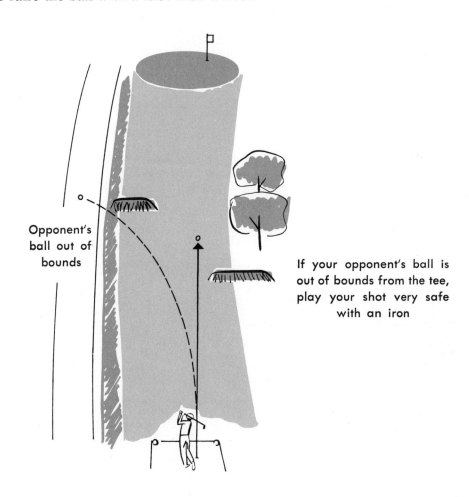

Opponent's
ball out of
bounds

If your opponent's ball is
out of bounds from the tee,
play your shot very safe
with an iron

(2) Low shots and hooks go together but for just the opposite reasons.

(3) Hooked shots tend to roll when they hit the ground; slices have more underspin and will stop more quickly.

(4) Don't depend on a deliberate hook shot from a close lie. To be certain of a hook, you must put the whole clubface on the ball. The slice, on the other hand, is fairly easy to execute from a close lie.

(5) If you bed the ball in rough, you'll have little chance of hitting a deliberate slice or hook. You'd best pitch the ball out safely and depend on your next shot.

For detailed discussion of these shots see HIGH SHOTS, HOOK SHOT, LOW SHOTS, PULLED SHOT, PUSHED SHOT and SLICE.

With ball embedded in rough, chances are against hitting either a slice or a hook at will

U

UNDERSWINGING: Underswinging (also known as "easing up" or "babying the shot") is not a common fault. The golfer who "kills the ball" may look to an easy swing for his cure. He forgets that a hard swing is still necessary for distance and accuracy.

Perhaps you feel that the club you've picked is a little too strong for the distance to be covered, so you ease up on the swing to guard against overshooting. This is the wrong approach to the problem. Pick out the right club to begin with and then hit the shot with crisp authority. Shorten the swing a bit if you feel you might go over the green with your club choice, but the same corrective rule for overswinging applies in this case: hit the ball with *controlled power*.

UNEVEN LIES: Uneven lies are situations in which one foot is higher than the other or the ball is on a different level than the feet. For specific discussions, see DOWNHILL LIES, SIDEHILL LIES and UPHILL LIES.

UPHILL LIES: When your right foot is on a lower level than your left, your main problem is shifting your weight quickly back to your left side at the start of the downswing. Put a little extra weight on your left side at the start of the backswing. You'll naturally tend to swing flat-footed and pull the shot off to the left, but you can overcome this tendency if you emphasize the weight shift back to your left side.

With any given club, you will hit the ball higher and shorter from an uphill lie than you would from a level lie. Always use a club at least one number lower than you would for a level shot of equal distance. (If you'd use a 5-iron under normal conditions, switch to a 4-iron.) If you're on a steep grade, choose a club two or more numbers lower.

Keep extra weight on left side. **Emphasize** weight shift to left side at start of downswing.

Uphill lie

On an uphill lie, you'll reach the bottom of your swing arc a shade later than you would under normal conditions. So position the ball about an inch nearer the left foot. During the first part of your follow-through let the clubhead follow the contour of the ground so you won't prod the turf and quit on the shot.

W

WAGGLE: Waggle is the name given the little series of preparatory movements made between the time you take your stance and begin your swing.

The waggle is the swing in miniature. It gives you the "feel" of the shot you are about to make, gets you into the rhythm of the swing and allows you time to check your grip, stance and aim.

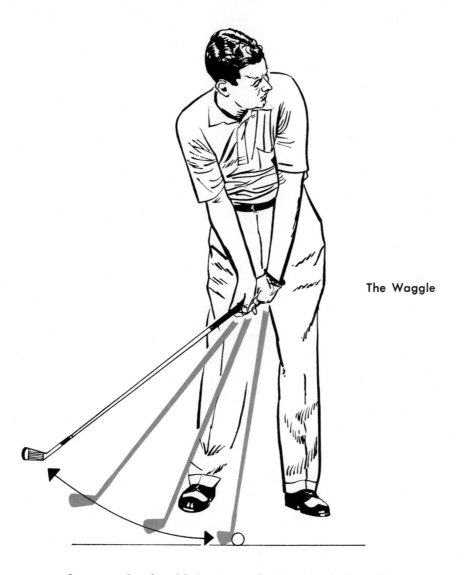

The Waggle

The waggle should be smooth, free and forceful. Your swing actually begins with the waggle, so you must concentrate on it. When you waggle back and forth along the intended line of flight, pay particular attention to the final six inches your clubhead must travel to meet the ball. If you waggle up and down—pick up the club abruptly and then set it back down behind the ball—you'll probably raise it abruptly on the backswing so that your stroke will be more of a chop than a swing.

A smooth, determined waggle won't insure a good over-all swing, but it will definitely help. If this preparatory wind-up is jerky or careless, you're reducing your chances of a good swing.

Also see PUTTING.

WARMUP: An important part of any round of golf is the brief warmup period that precedes it. It is patently foolish to start a round with stiff muscles.

Thirty or forty shots should suffice. Too many swings may tire you before the actual round is over. Start with a few easy practice swings to loosen up. Then hit a few with the short irons, work up through the medium and long irons and then the woods. When you've warmed up with the driver, go back to one of the short irons and hit three or four short pitches to taper off.

The warmup serves two purposes: (1) It loosens up the muscles. And (2) it enables you to check up on your swing.

During the first part of the warmup—say the first ten balls—concentrate on timing the swing properly and catching the ball solidly with the middle of the clubface. Swing slowly and easily. Then check for errors in grip, stance, posture, takeaway and downswing—the fundamentals. Finally, concentrate on some particular fault, such as slicing or hooking.

Complete the warmup with a dozen or so practice putts. Tune up your touch on approach putts. Then tap in a few short ones to perfect

During the first part of the warm-up, swing slowly and easily, concentrate on timing

If you dig in too far on soggy turf, you are apt to get your face spattered with mud and water, causing you to flinch thereafter during the round on similar shots. Good results are not likely to follow when you flinch on the shot.

your putting. Before you step up to the first tee, hit two or three very long approach putts.

WEATHER: Following are suggestions for meeting specific situations arising from showers and extremes of temperature. Wind problems are given special consideration under WIND.

WET WEATHER

A spot of water between clubface and ball makes a lot of difference in the way the ball travels. The effect of the groove markings is nullified. (As we have seen in the section on CLUBS, these grooves make the ball hew to the line.)

When you hit a ball out of wet grass, you're using in effect an ungrooved club. The wobbly shot that results resembles a knuckleball thrown by a baseball pitcher—*i.e.*, the spin is erratic.

There are two things you can do to help overcome this hazard: (*1*) Try to hit the ball as cleanly as possible to minimize the water's effect. And (*2*) use the margins of safety that are available to you.

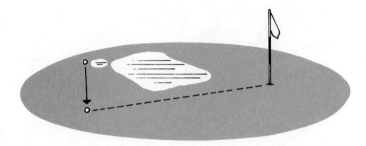

The "casual water" rule permits the player to move his ball without penalty to avoid putting through any temporary puddles of water on the green

(On iron shots, play for the "fat" part of the green, and steer clear of traps and other obstacles.)

If you dig in too far in the soggy turf, you'll spatter your face with mud and water. This could lead to flinching later in the round.

Putting on wet greens: You'll find that sidehill putts break less on water-logged greens than on dry greens. That's because the ball travels *through* the soft, wet grass (*see* PUTTING). Then too, wet greens are slower than dry ones. So you can afford to be bold when you putt.

CASUAL WATER RULE

More golfers should familiarize themselves with the provisions of the United States Golf Association rule covering casual water. While most players know that they can remove the ball without penalty from a temporary puddle of water, not all of them understand why.

On the green, for instance, the player can move the ball without penalty to avoid having to putt *through* a puddle. The provisions also state that you can move the ball so you won't have to stand in casual water. And if the water interferes with your swing, you can move the ball. If you lose a ball under a condition cited by the casual water rule, you may drop another ball "as near as possible to the place where the ball entered the area, on ground which avoids these conditions."

COLD WEATHER

In cold weather dress for comfort and freedom of movement. Be

Shirt and
light knit
sweater

In cold weather, dress so as not
to hamper your freedom of
movement in the shoulders

sure you have plenty of freedom through the shoulders. It's better to wear two or more layers of clothes than something thick.

Those little handwarmers used by the duck hunting set really come in handy. They not only keep your hands warm, but you can stick a couple of spare golf balls in the pocket. Remember, a ball performs best at a temperature of 87 degrees; it will go 10-20 yards farther off the tee than a "cold" ball. So change to a warm ball on each hole.

HOT WEATHER

When you play in extremely hot weather, pace yourself so you won't be fagged out on the finishing holes. Rest while your opponents and partner are making their shots. If you exert yourself needlessly, you'll be in poor shape for a strong finish.

Use salt tablets on extremely hot days. You can get them for free at most golf courses.

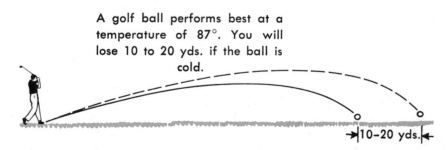

A golf ball performs best at a
temperature of 87°. You will
lose 10 to 20 yds. if the ball is
cold.

10–20 yds.

Pace yourself in hot weather so that you won't be exhausted on the finishing holes

If you're wearing a full-finger golf glove on a hot day, remove it occasionally so it won't become slippery with perspiration.

WILDNESS: *See* SPRAYING

WIND: How does the wind affect a golf ball in flight? Too many players oversimplify the problems of wind play. They consider a very low shot ideal when you're playing into the wind, and for a following wind they think only in terms of a high shot. These logical concepts neglect the ball's angle of descent.

HEADWINDS

A shot hit low into the wind continues to rise gradually until its power is spent, then drops directly. This shot is often called a "wind-cheater," though the phrase should really apply to the high shot that

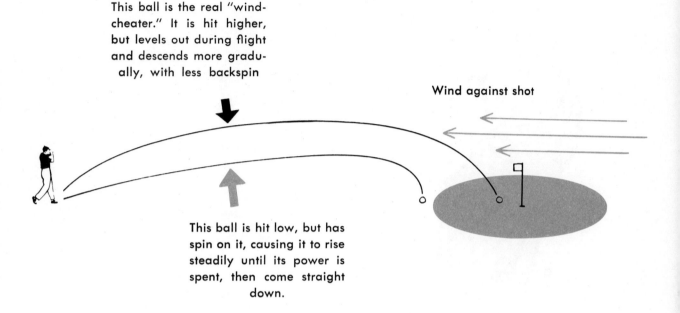

This ball is the real "wind-cheater." It is hit higher, but levels out during flight and descends more gradually, with less backspin

Wind against shot

This ball is hit low, but has spin on it, causing it to rise steadily until its power is spent, then come straight down.

Which ball is the wind-cheater?

levels out in mid-flight and descends more gradually. The former shot has more spin.

When you play in the wind, particularly an adverse wind, try to avoid excessive spin. The smaller the amount of spin, the better your control on all wind shots. And you'll add a lot of distance on shots hit into the wind.

To avoid spin, put as much of the clubface on the ball as possible —*i.e.*, hit it as solidly as you can. For proper balance and rhythm (timing), swing well within your maximum power. Keep your head still and your eye on the back of the ball.

You've probably heard that you should swing more easily than usual when playing into the wind. Remember that your effort to swing easily is offset by a natural tendency to overswing into the wind. What you really want is a perfectly natural power swing.

The wind accentuates whatever underspin and side spin you put on the ball. That's why slices and hooks are sharper in the wind. Also,

To keep extra spin off the ball, get as much of the clubface on the ball at contact as possible. This means hitting the ball as solidly as possible.

the ball stays in the air longer over a shorter distance when the wind is blowing against it and the curve is accentuated.

Poor wind shots result when you try to obtain as much distance against the wind as you would without it. This is particularly true of the driver.

Most of the problems in wind play are psychological. At address and throughout the swing, advanced golfers tend to keep more weight than usual on the left heel. This shortens the swing so that you don't arc the ball too quickly. You hit straight through the ball instead of against it.

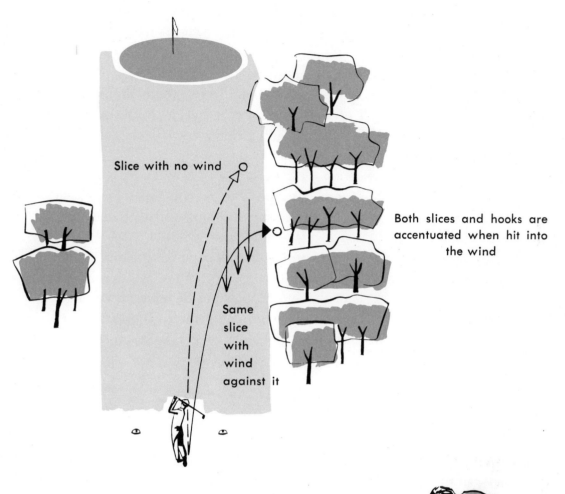

Slice with no wind

Both slices and hooks are accentuated when hit into the wind

Same slice with wind against it

The only physical adjustment of proven worth for a wind shot: Keep more weight on the left heel throughout the swing

The player who allows for habitual slices and hooks is at an added disadvantage in the wind. He must realize that adverse winds increase the curves of flight.

Don't tee the ball lower than normal. You want the ball up high enough for solid impact. The low tee induces a more pronounced downward blow instead of the desired level sweep. And you'll get more spin. Don't tee the ball too high either or you'll club the ball on the underside.

I'm concluding this section with examples of how to play various clubs against winds of 10 and 20 mph. By 10-mph I'm referring to winds that vary from "light" to "brisk"; a 20-mph wind is a strong wind. The techniques used to play into strong winds applies also to slightly slower winds and gusts up to 30-mph. And for greater winds, the same general principles apply.

At 10-mph the wind is of definite though not decisive importance. At 20-mph and over the wind is a determining force. You can detect the wind's force by tossing up some blades of grass. *Any* noticeable wind affects the ball in flight to some extent.

Situation: Drive into a 10-mph wind.

Solution: Tee the ball at normal height. No particular physical adjustments are needed for drives into winds of 10 mph or less. Concentrate on making a controlled power swing and catching the ball solidly in the center of the clubface. A drive that would go 230 yards without an effective wind will be reduced by approximately 15 yards. Any slice or hook will be accentuated to some extent. Figure on a small loss of yardage and don't try to make it up by swinging harder. If the layout of the hole permits it, give yourself a little extra safety margin. The wind will blow a slice or hook farther off the intended line of flight than would otherwise be the case.

Situation: Fairway wood shots into a 10-mph wind.

Solution: Use the normal stance and swing. Your choice of club (2, 3 or 4-wood) is important. A good index is to choose the number below the club you'd use if there were no wind. A wind of this speed will cut down on distance enough to make this sliding rule valid. With a slightly less lofted club you can lift the ball more easily against the

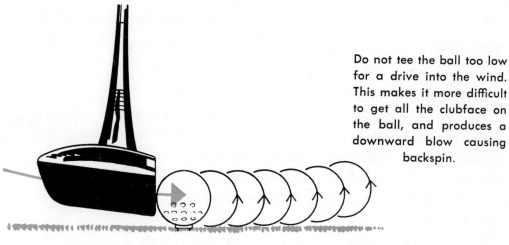

Do not tee the ball too low for a drive into the wind. This makes it more difficult to get all the clubface on the ball, and produces a downward blow causing backspin.

Winds up to 20 miles-an-hour should definitely be considered in playing a shot, but are not the dominant factor

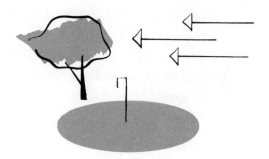

Winds above 20 miles-an-hour are the dominant factor in playing the shot

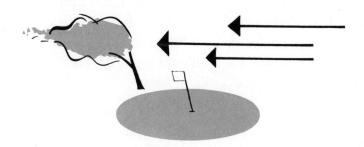

215 yds.   230 yds.
(no wind)

Drive into 10 mile-an-hour wind will be cut back about 15 yds.

wind. You can use an extra margin of safety wherever possible, since an adverse wind will accentuate the curve ever so slightly.

Situation: Long-iron shots into a 10-mph wind.

Solution: Use the same stance and swing you'd normally use and the next lower club. Swing with controlled power, and concentrate on meeting the ball solidly. Remember that a wood club will give you more face than a long iron. When in doubt as to your choice of club, choose the longer one. If you're afraid of too much distance, cut down on your power a bit.

Situation: Medium-iron shots into a 10-mph wind.

Solution: Use the normal stance and swing and the next longer club than you'd ordinarily choose. As you reach the medium iron range, a ball hit into the wind descends at a sharp angle. You won't have to worry about the ball stopping after it hits, but watch out for sand traps. A ball coming straight down is likely to bury itself in the sand.

Situation: Short-iron shots into a 10-mph wind.

Solution: Use the normal stance and swing and the next longer club. If in doubt, shorten your swing. Never press this shot. The angle of descent is quite sharp in this club range, especially with the 9-iron and pitching wedge. The ball is likely to roll backward after hitting on a level green or one that slopes toward you. You can judge the distance more easily if you can count on the ball's rolling a few feet (no more) after it strikes the green.

Situation: Short pitches and chip shots into a 10-mph wind.

Solution: The wind blowing toward you will simplify your problem

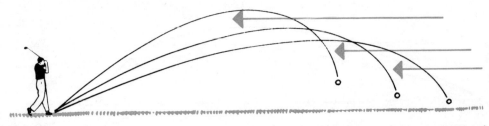

5 Iron   2 Iron   2 Wood

Against a 10 mile-an-hour wind: { Use a 2 Wood instead of a 3 Wood
Use a 2 Iron instead of a 3 Iron
Use a 5 Iron instead of a 6 Iron

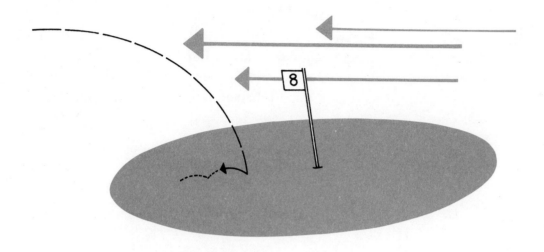

9 Iron or Pitching Wedge hit into
a 10 mile-an-hour wind is apt
to roll backwards after hitting
green

by cutting down on the roll. No swing or stance adjustments are necessary. Since the wind won't affect distance and roll much, rely on your sense of touch. Use the club you'd normally select.

Situation: Drive into a 20-mph wind.

Solution: When the wind reaches this general speed range, it determines the kind of shot you must make. You must adjust to an anticipated loss of 15-40 yards on full shots. You'll tend to overswing more. Plant your feet firmly in the ground with your weight through the heels to insure proper balance throughout the swing—a strong wind can easily make you sway. Concentrate on meeting the ball solidly. Take advantage of whatever safety margins are available, since winds of this range will greatly accentuate any slice or hook. Position the ball as you normally would, but be extra careful not to place the ball too far in front of you so that you pick up additional height.

Situation: Fairway wood shots into a 20-mph wind.

Solution: The same general principles that apply to fairway wood shots into winds of 10-mph also hold true for 20-mph winds. Your

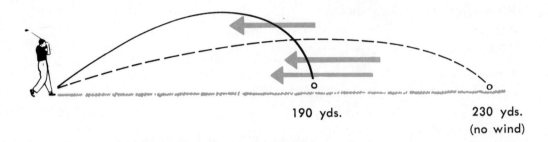

190 yds.   230 yds.
                            (no wind)

Drive into a wind of 20 miles-an-hour or more will sometimes lose
as much as 40 yards in distance

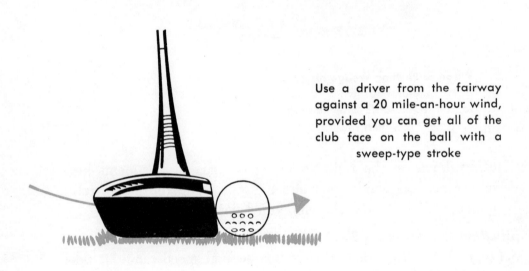

Use a driver from the fairway
against a 20 mile-an-hour wind,
provided you can get all of the
club face on the ball with a
sweep-type stroke

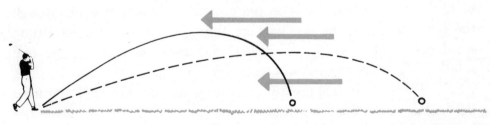

3 Iron into 20 mph. wind   3 Iron with no wind

On a long iron shot into a 20 mile-an-hour wind, the club choice
will be two clubs longer, possibly even three.

driver becomes a fairway wood when you have an exceptionally good lie or when, as is often the case, you are playing winter rules and can obtain a good lie.* Place your driver directly behind the ball to see if you can get all of the clubface on the ball with a sweeping stroke. If so, your driver may be the right club. A wind coming at you will help lift the ball. Because your driver is a straighter faced club, it can give you added distance in this situation by lowering the ball's normal trajectory and reducing the amount of spin. This stratagem is not for beginners, but it can prove helpful to more experienced players when not overdone.

Situation: Long-iron shots into a 20-mph wind.

Solution: Swing well within your maximum power. Place a little extra weight on your left heel to guard against overswinging (you'll shorten your swing slightly). Choose a club that's two and possibly three clubs longer than the one you'd normally pick. Resolve all doubts in favor of a longer club. Never press this decision. Shots of considerable height will drop straight down and stop quickly. So be careful to avoid sand traps.

Situation: Medium-iron shots into a 20-mph wind.

Solution: Apply the same general principles that hold for the medium irons in a 10-mph wind, only place a little more weight on your left heel so you can shorten your swing. Your club is two numbers higher instead of one. Hit well within your maximum power. Steer clear of sand traps, since balls hit into winds of this strength will fall straight down and plunge deeply into the sand.

Situation: Short-iron shots into a 20-mph wind.

Solution: Avoid full shots with the 7, 8 and 9-iron and the pitching wedge, *particularly* the 9-iron and pitching wedge, which will deliver high wild shots with little forward power. Choose a stronger club and shorten your stroke. You should regard your 6-iron as a short rather than a medium iron. Shorten your swing a bit to cut down on distance

---

* The face lift of a standard driver is 11 degrees as compared with 14 degrees for the 2-wood, 16 degrees for the 3-wood and 19 degrees for the 4-wood. The major club characteristics are treated more fully under CLUBS. I merely cite these figures to show that it's reasonable to use a driver from exceptionally good lies in the fairway when the wind is blowing toward you.

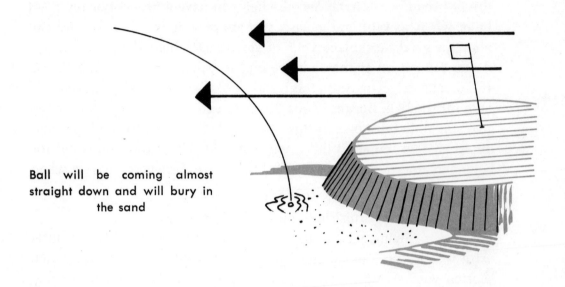

Ball will be coming almost
straight down and will bury in
the sand

Give sand traps a wide berth on a medium iron shot into a wind
of 20 miles-an-hour

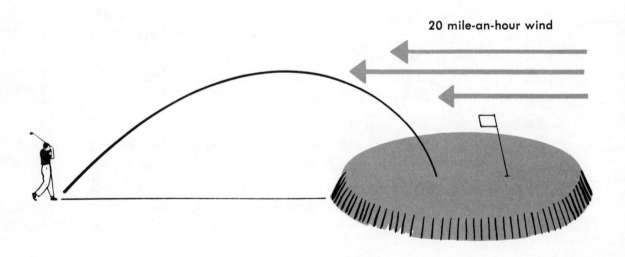

20 mile-an-hour wind

From about 120 yds. out, use a 6 Iron as a short iron for a full shot
into a strong wind

and use the 6-iron for shots of 120 yards or so to keep the ball down and send it forward.

Situation: Pitch shots into a 20-mph wind.

Solution: For a shot of 30 to 70 yards or so into a strong wind, a 7 or 8-iron is preferable to the 9-iron or pitching wedge. The shot requires a certain amount of forward power to make the ball hold its line through the wind. It's no problem to stop the ball. On a 60-yard shot, the 8-iron does the same work as the pitching wedge would with no contending wind. If you were to use the pitching wedge against a strong wind, it would be equivalent—under normal conditions—to using a club deeper than any you carry.

Situation: Chip shots into a 20-mph wind.

Solution: Even a wind this brisk makes little difference when you enter this close a range. But remember that the wind will affect these shots just as it does the longer ones. Your shot will drop more directly and thus stop more quickly. Also, if the chip is a fairly long one (say 25 or 30 yards), the wind will slow it in flight.

20 mile-an-hour wind

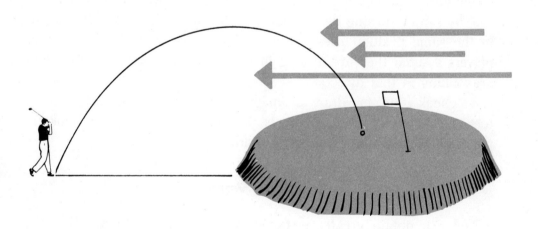

On a pitch shot of 30 to 70 yds., use a 7 or 8 Iron instead of a 9 Iron or Pitching Wedge

CROSSWINDS

Crosswinds affect your aim. Some better players try to hold a shot straight against a right-to-left wind by deliberately cutting across the ball slightly to give it a fading action. Playing into a left-to-right wind, they'll impart a slight hook spin to the ball. These complications are unnecessary. Simply line up your shot in accordance with the amount of drift you can expect. You won't need a table, and as a matter of fact, there "ain't no such animal"—conditions are too variable.

Right or left drift will affect all shots from woods to short irons in the same degree. This is because the long shots have a lot of forward power to begin with and are hardly affected until near the end of their flight while the short shots, which have less power and more spin, are more easily diverted. However, the long shots are affected by the wind over a greater distance.

The right-handed player—especially one who tends to hook the ball—finds it easy to drive into a right-to-left crosswind. But the left-to-right wind poses a difficult problem for him. He's got to line up the shot and execute it with unusual care.

Check the position of your feet, hips and shoulders in relation to the intended line of flight. Some golfers try to line up a crosswind shot by simply turning their shoulders slightly while their feet remain in the same position used for a straight-away shot. In fact, some players assume they are aiming in a certain direction because they are looking in that direction.

To check your aim, draw an imaginary line from an object to your feet. This method of lining up is particularly effective for hookers playing into a strong left-to-right wind.

FOLLOWING WINDS

You can obtain greater distance and accuracy with a following wind than you can bucking an adverse wind. A good brisk following wind will cut down slices and hooks and add to the player's confidence, especially on long shots. Most golfers are at their best with a nice wind at their backs.

All full shots will be affected to about the same degree by a given wind from right to left

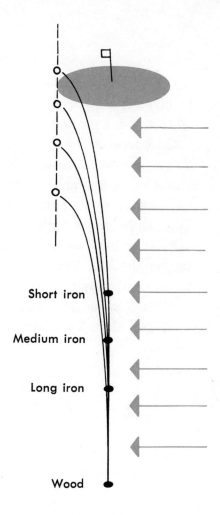

Short iron

Medium iron

Long iron

Wood

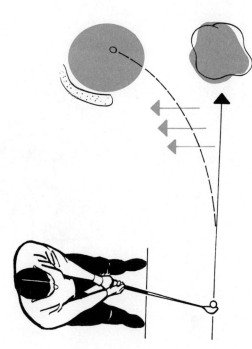

Line up on a tree to the right of the green for a shot into a cross wind from right to left. The wind will carry the ball into the green

Use your normal swing in a mild following wind. You don't have to make special adjustments to lift the ball high. The wind speed 50 feet above ground is no greater than it is 20 feet above.

On iron shots to the green, don't try to add underspin to the ball to cut down the roll unless you're confronted by traps or other obstacles. It is much better to try to hit the shot with no more than the normal amount of spin and allow for a normal amount of roll. You can judge your distance much more easily that way.

Most golfers believe that the stronger the following wind, the farther the ball will travel. This is not true and has led to a lot of incorrect thinking.

A wind speed of 15 to 20 mph will produce the maximum carry on a golf shot. To understand why, turn to the section on adverse

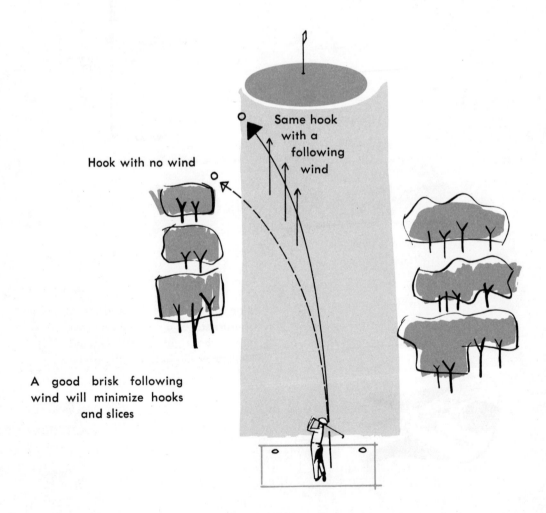

Hook with no wind

Same hook
with a
following
wind

A good brisk following
wind will minimize hooks
and slices

Wind produces a leveling action on the ball

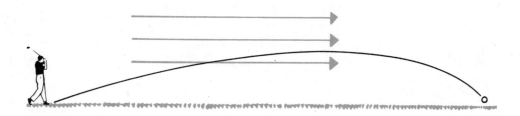

A following wind speed of 15 to 20 miles-an-hour will produce
maximum carry on a golf shot

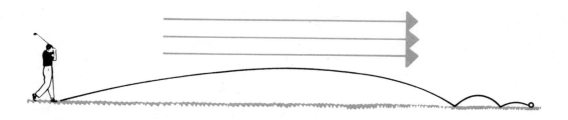

Strong following winds over 20 miles-an-hour will cut down on
carry, never allowing the shot to really get up in the air

winds and see how they help get the ball airborne. The following
wind keeps the ball down because it tends to level the ball's flight
in conformity with the wind's own movement.

Winds up to 20-mph carry the ball sufficiently far to offset any
distance lost through this leveling action. But in very strong winds,
the leveling action keeps the ball down and reduces carry.

You must take the leveling action into account when judging your
shot. Your estimate of the ball's roll must depend on the texture of the
ground where the ball will hit and the length and thickness of the
grass.

To get a good carry, you must hit the ball with enough power to
lift it through the wind to a proper height. So be wary of underclubbing when a strong wind is behind you and you need lots of
distance in the air.

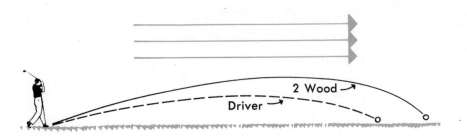

In a strong following wind over 20 miles-an-hour, a 2 Wood or a
3 Wood will usually produce more carry off the tee

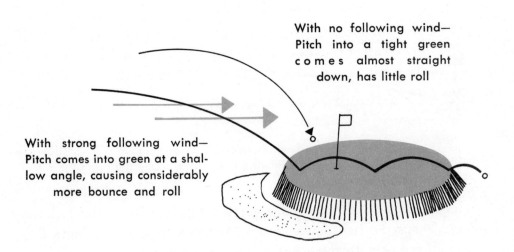

With no following wind—
Pitch into a tight green
comes almost straight
down, has little roll

With strong following wind—
Pitch comes into green at a shallow angle, causing considerably
more bounce and roll

This brings up a question: when the wind is following, will a
2-wood or 3-wood give you more distance off the tee than the driver?
In winds up to 20-mph, no; in stronger winds, yes. Much depends
on the way the ball is hit. A player who habitually hits a low ball
might be well advised to take a more lofted wood in 15-mile winds
while a high ball hitter should stick to the driver through winds of
twice that speed.

While a following wind is a big help in attaining distance, it is a
considerable handicap on less-than-full shots into the green. This
handicap is most pronounced on holes where the green is guarded by

traps or elevated on all sides so that the only approach is by air. Here the angle of descent comes strongly into play. When there's a following wind, the angle is gradual and conducive to roll. The best way to solve this problem is to place the shot properly before you approach the green so that you'll have the greatest amount of space in which to stop the ball.

The shot that will stop quickest under the conditions outlined above is the full pitching wedge, which sends the ball high enough for a sharp angle of descent and gives it a lot of underspin. A shot that's not full is likely to have a lower trajectory and less underspin. On a full shot there's maximum friction between the clubface grooves and the ball. For this reason it's often wise to make a shorter tee shot when you see that the second shot should stop quickly on the green.

On full iron shots into the green, don't use a club with too much loft or press for extra distance. A compact, controlled power swing with the right club gives you the best stopping action. This stroke permits the clubface grooves to produce the underspin action for which they are designed.

Situation: Drive with a following wind.

Solution: Some players try to set distance records in a following wind and end up overswinging. This upsets rhythm and timing— the player hits the ball off center and loses accuracy and distance.

With a following wind behind you on the tee, **don't** try to set distance records. This will cause overswinging and usually a missed shot.

Other players wax overconfident: driving with the wind looks like a pipe. Swing as you ordinarily would. Try to hit the ball solidly. The following wind will minimize slices and hooks by keeping the ball on line, but you should remain alert to the advantages of this temporary condition.

Situation: Fairway wood shot with a following wind.

Solution: Watch out that you don't pick a 2-wood for a 3-wood or a 3 for a 4-wood. When in doubt, choose the deeper of the two woods in question. The idea is to get the ball up and away. A solid 4-wood hit will give you more distance than a 2-wood hit slightly off center. In this situation you must get the ball airborne. Use the same stance and swing you would for any fairway wood play.

Situation: Long iron shot with a following wind.

Solution: The big problem here is judging distance. A solidly hit 2-iron shot of normal height may travel 50 to 60 yards farther than one hit slightly off center that fails to rise with normal speed. So you've got to be careful. It's difficult to make the ball stop quickly after it hits. A crisp, solid blow with a controlled power swing gives the best results. Your stance and swing are the same you'd use for the long iron shot when the wind is negligible.

Situation: Medium iron shot with a following wind.

Solution: Again, a shot hit slightly off center, imparting side spin, will travel a much shorter distance. A frequent fault is going for too much distance with a particular club simply because you're afraid that a stronger club plus the wind would carry the ball past your

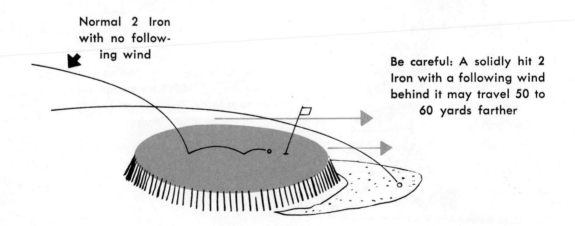

Normal 2 Iron
with no follow-
ing wind

Be careful: A solidly hit 2
Iron with a following wind
behind it may travel 50 to
60 yards farther

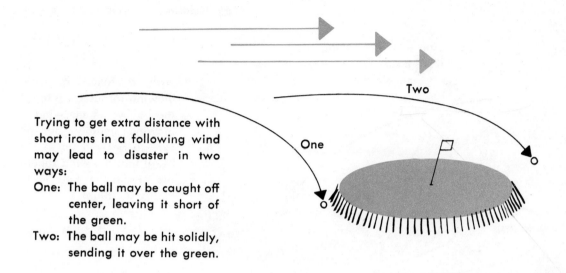

Trying to get extra distance with short irons in a following wind may lead to disaster in two ways:

One: The ball may be caught off center, leaving it short of the green.

Two: The ball may be hit solidly, sending it over the green.

objective. You can count on the wind to add to your carry (about 10 yards in a 10-mile wind), but the flight pattern is the same as you could expect for no wind.

Situation: Short iron shot with a following wind.

Solution: Your striking pattern must be consistent if you're going to gauge distance with any accuracy. Don't try for extra distance with your short irons in a following wind. If you overswing and happen to catch the ball squarely, you may get considerably more distance than you'd bargained for. But the usual fault is to catch the ball off center and place it far short of the objective. Again, it's not easy to make the ball stop after it hits.

A controlled power swing is best. Catch the ball on its underside and hit straight through.

Situation: Pitch shots and chip shots with a following wind.

Solution: Virtually all pitch shots before a following wind should be made with the pitching wedge. This club will give you the greatest height, angle of descent and underspin—all of which you need on pitch and chip shots with the wind. The techniques of shooting are the same you'd use if there were no wind.

For chip shots, choose the next deeper club from the one you'd ordinarily use. A following wind on this short shot cuts down loft and adds to the roll to the same extent as the next shallower club would.

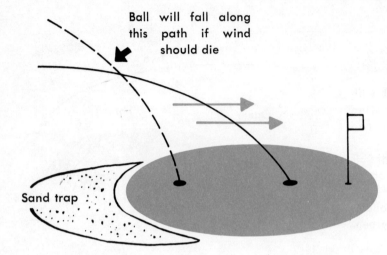

Ball will fall along this path if wind should die

With a following wind blowing in gusts, try to hit the ball when the wind is blowing steadily, but be sure to be well up in the event that the wind should die while the ball is in flight

Sand trap

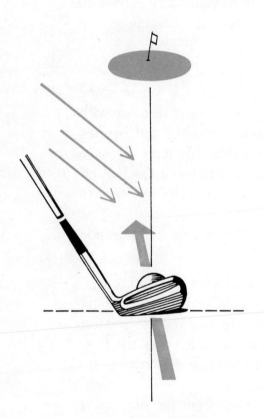

If the wind is quartering against you from the left, close the clubface slightly

If the wind is quartering against you from the right, open the clubface slightly

Situation: Shooting when the wind is blowing in gusts.

Solution: All you can do is try to latch onto an instant when the wind is blowing with steady force and play the shot as safely as possible. When your greatest danger is overshooting the green, play a shot that's not calculated to go too far. When you're in danger of falling short of the green, try to extend your shot for height or distance.

QUARTERING WINDS

When the wind is quartering against you from the left—*i.e.,* blowing back and across the line of flight—close the clubface a degree or two; if it's quartering from the right, open the clubface several degrees. This adjustment is very slight, and you must make it before you grip the club. If the club is toed in or out for a straightaway shot, it will revert to a square position during the swing.

You need only make a slight adjustment in aim in a quartering wind from behind.

WOODS: *See* CLUBS

Index